INSIGHT GUIDES

GREAT BREAKS
EDINBURGH

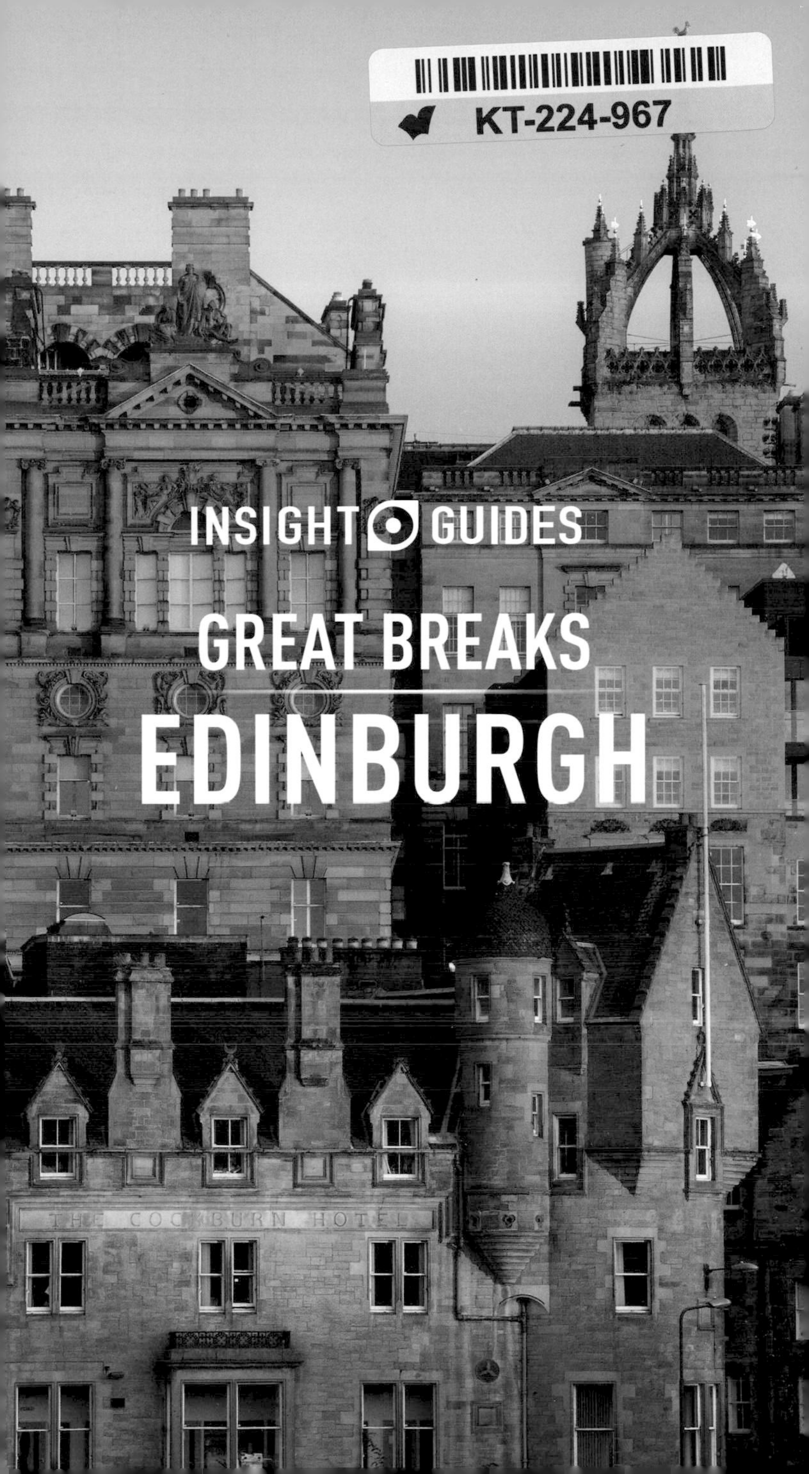

Walking Eye App

YOUR FREE EBOOK AVAILABLE THROUGH THE WALKING EYE APP

Your guide now includes a free eBook to your chosen destination, for the same great price as before. Simply download the Walking Eye App from the App Store or Google Play to access your free eBook.

HOW THE WALKING EYE APP WORKS

Through the Walking Eye App, you can purchase a range of eBooks and destination content. However, when you buy this book, you can download the corresponding eBook for free. Just see below in the grey panel where to find your free content and then scan the QR code at the bottom of this page.

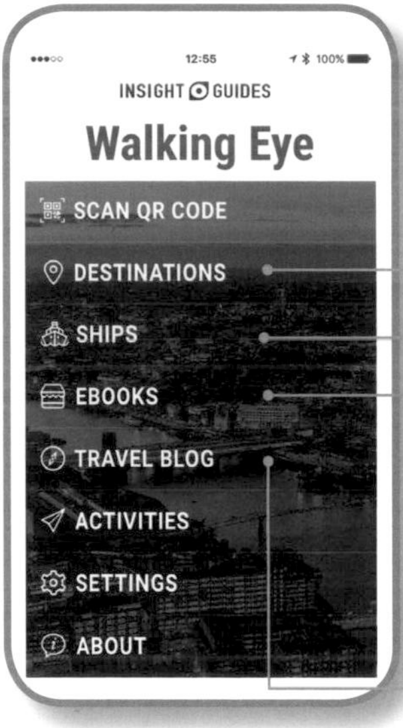

Destinations: Download essential destination content featuring recommended sights and attractions, restaurants, hotels and an A–Z of practical information, all available for purchase.

Ships: Interested in ship reviews? Find independent reviews of river and ocean ships in this section, all available for purchase.

eBooks: You can download your free accompanying digital version of this guide here. You will also find a whole range of other eBooks, all available for purchase.

Free access to travel-related blog articles about different destinations, updated on a daily basis.

HOW THE EBOOKS WORK

The eBooks are provided in EPUB file format. Please note that you will need an eBook reader installed on your device to open the file. Many devices come with this as standard, but you may still need to install one manually from Google Play.

The eBook content is identical to the content in the printed guide.

HOW TO DOWNLOAD THE WALKING EYE APP

1. Download the Walking Eye App from the App Store or Google Play.
2. Open the app and select the scanning function from the main menu.
3. Scan the QR code on this page – you will then be asked a security question to verify ownership of the book.
4. Once this has been verified, you will see your eBook in the purchased ebook section, where you will be able to download it.

Other destination apps and eBooks are available for purchase separately or are free with the purchase of the Insight Guide book.

GET IT ON Google Play

Download on the App Store

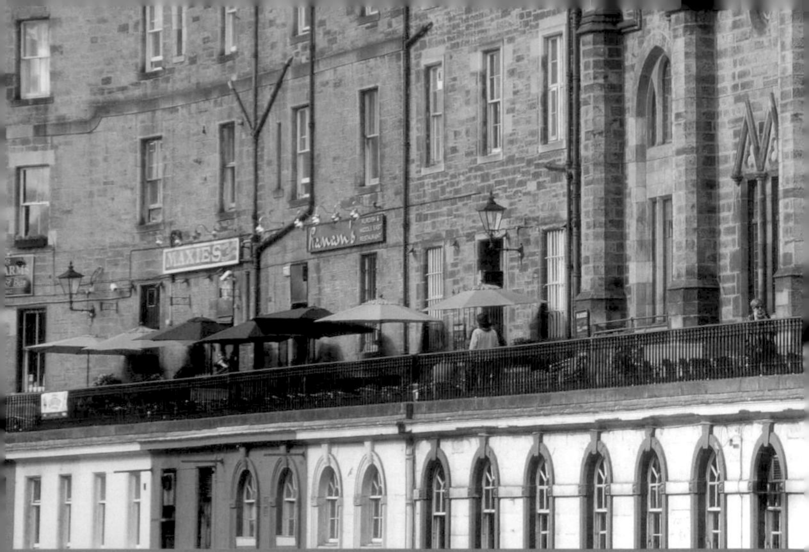

Contents

Travel Tips

Edinburgh's Top 10

From its impressive castle and elegant Georgian architecture to its world-class museums and cutting-edge arts festival, here, at a glance, are the top attractions of the fascinating Scottish capital

▲ **Edinburgh Castle.** This imposing and impenetrable fortress defines Scottish history and is visible from every corner of the city. See page 23.

▲ **The Royal Mile.** A stunning stretch of cobblestones, medieval passageways, churches and museums leads down to the Palace of Holyroodhouse. See page 28.

▲ **The Festival.** The world descends on Edinburgh in August to take part in a vast celebration of the arts, with thousands of comedy, theatre and literary events. See page 60.

▶ **Literary Edinburgh.** Explore the city that spawned *Sherlock Holmes*, *Peter Pan*, *Treasure Island*, *Harry Potter* and *Trainspotting*. See page 42.

▲ **Calton Hill.** This volcanic outcrop crowned with monuments has panoramic views of the city, Holyrood Palace and the Firth of Forth. See page 67.

▲ **New Town architecture.** Designed between 1740 and 1850, the neoclassical city's crescents and terraces are a triumph of Georgian architecture. See page 72.

▲ **National Museum of Scotland.** Recounts Scottish history with national treasures and multimedia displays. See page 53.

▼ **City art.** Among an unprecedented 30 galleries in central Edinburgh are four housing the National Collection, in which pride of place must go to the Scottish National Gallery. See page 63.

▼ **The Scottish Parliament Building.** A complex yet stunning award-winning design that shocks and pleases in equal measure. See page 39.

▼ **Royal Botanic Garden.** This world-famous garden dates back to 1670 and houses a vast selection of beautiful, exotic plants. See page 86.

View of St Andrew's House from Calton Hill.

Overview

An Enlightened Capital

Far beyond its label as the host of Britain's biggest cultural festival, Edinburgh is also its most visually impressive city with a history and charm that few others can rival

Declared a Unesco World Heritage Site in 1995, the centre of Edinburgh is a fascinating juxtaposition of medieval confusion and classical architectural harmony. The higgledy-piggledy Old Town, built around the Castle on a volcanic plug where the first defensive settlement was founded over 2,000 years ago, contrasts remarkably with the New Town – in fact now more than 200 years old – where order and harmony prevail within the largest area of Georgian architecture ever conceived. Today, the city is the capital of an ancient nation whose influence resonates around the globe. It has a proud history of artistic excellence, intellectual endeavour and scientific discovery that is reflected in its national confidence and devolved parliament. The Edinburgh Festival, tripling the city's half a million or so inhabitants each August, is its flagship event, but all year round a selection of great museums, beautiful parks and vibrant entertainment make it one of Europe's most exciting destinations.

LANDSCAPE AND CLIMATE

Strategically situated inland from the southern shore of the Firth of Forth, an estuary of the North Sea on Scotland's east coast, the capital, like Rome, lies on seven hills. Rising above Princes Street, the main shopping thoroughfare, the castle rock is the start of the Royal Mile, the Old Town backbone. Stretching down to the Palace of Holyroodhouse, there is further dramatic scenery in the form of Arthur's Seat, another extinct volcano surrounded by rocky crags and lush parkland. To the north, between the castle and the Port of Leith on the Firth of Forth, sprawls the New Town, where in just one square mile (2.5 sq km) thousands of buildings are listed for their architectural merit.

The weather on Scotland's west coast is wetter than on the east, but Edinburgh is notorious for the seasonal North Sea 'haar', a mist that periodically settles over the city. When it does rain, a strong wind sometimes renders umbrellas useless. Generally, summers are moderately warm, and winters are cold but clear, with occasional light snowfall. For most of the year the climate makes for more of an indoor, than outdoor, existence, and locals, for the most part, tend to go about their everyday lives immune to the weather. When the sun does

Edinburgh Military Tattoo.

The People of Edinburgh

The citizens of Edinburgh have a reputation for being reserved and prim, no doubt as much due to the city's 19th-century banking and insurance boom (contrasting with Glasgow's heavy industry) as it was to its 17th-century adoption of Calvinist Protestantism. There's a saying that while 'breeding' in Glasgow is thought of as good fun, 'breeding' in Edinburgh is considered good form. This jibe holds no truth and merely underlines the two cities' lasting rivalry.

come out, however, the city is transformed, the population taking full advantage of its many green spaces.

A RICH HISTORY

Edinburgh evolved from the 6th century onwards with the merging of Pictish and Celtic kingdoms, together with Saxon, Norman and even Viking influences. In 1124 David I became King of Scotland and set about building feudalism and Christian monasteries with support from his Norman friends. Within a few centuries, Edinburgh was well established as Scotland's capital with a burgeoning professional class. A harsh blow to the people's self-esteem was dealt in 1707 by the Act of Union – with monarch and parliament based 400 miles (644km) away in London – but Scotland retained its own Church, legislature and law (based unlike England on the Roman Law tradition), which helped to preserve a Scottish identity. Nonetheless, the feeling that Edinburgh had become a hollow capital persisted until the end of the 20th century, when a Scottish parliament was elected.

The Scottish Enlightenment during the 18th and 19th centuries was Edinburgh's finest hour, drawing together many of the greatest minds in Europe. In a tavern off the Royal Mile, David Hume, who wrote a six-volume history of England, held court with the physician William Cullen, the chemist Joseph Black, the mathematician John Playfair, the dramatist John Home, the first sociologist Adam Ferguson, and the first capitalist economist Adam Smith – and by the end of this golden age Sir Walter Scott's novels had become European bestsellers. Painters such as Henry Raeburn, Allan Ramsay, Jr, and David Wilkie documented the age, while the Adam family dazzled the nation with architectural achievement. With the University of Edinburgh founded in 1583 and three more universities in the 20th century, the city has always been a centre of intellectual excellence, hosting a large student population.

Edinburgh is today a financial centre of international standing, founded on traditional virtues of prudence and propriety that were shaken in only a minor way by the 2008 gov-

One of Edinburgh's narrow wynds.

One of several excellent chocolate shops in the city.

ernment bailout of the Bank of Scotland, founded in 1695. This eminence shouldn't surprise: it was a Scotsman, after all (William Paterson), who founded the Bank of England, while Adam Smith's 1776 masterwork *The Wealth of Nations* championed the paradox of private gain yielding public good – something Edinburgh's lawyers and accountants took seriously, making fortunes from investment overseas.

FOOD AND DRINK

Edinburgh offers a vast range of food, from excellent Scottish fare to French, Italian, Thai or Indian. Scotland's fish and meat are among the best in the world, including wild salmon, sea bass and scallops, Aberdeen Angus beef, venison and game birds from Highland estates as well as regional cheeses. With some of the very best restaurants in Britain, most establishments concentrate on serving these wonderful ingredients with a modern, international accent.

The Scottish national dish, haggis, consists of lamb's heart and liver mixed with suet, oats and spices, and is traditionally boiled in the sheep's stomach lining (a vegetarian alternative is available). Generally eaten with mashed swede and potato ('neeps and tatties'), haggis is also sometimes incorporated into a starter.

Scottish breakfasts are a veritable feast, with eggs, bacon, sausages, porridge, Scottish-smoked kipper or haddock and black pudding. That's how the day should start, and it should end with a nip of Scotch whisky or a pint of dark ale. In Edinburgh pubs, try the Caledonian Edinburgh Castle 80-shilling ale from the local brewery.

As souvenirs to take home, high-quality Scottish products such as marmalade, oatcakes, shortbread and smoked salmon can be readily purchased at delicatessens, and the selection of finest single-malt Scotch whiskies is larger here than anywhere else in the world.

Find our recommended restaurants at the end of each tour. Below is a Price Guide to help you make your choice.

Eating Out Price Guide

Two-course meal for one person, including a glass of wine.

£££ = over £30
££ = £20–30
£ = under £20

Guide to Coloured Boxes

Eating
Fact
Green
Kids
Shopping
View

This guide is dotted with coloured boxes providing additional practical and cultural information to make the most of your visit. Here is a guide to the coding system.

Entertainment

While Edinburgh's Festivals (see page 60) provide the high points of the entertainment calendar, the city's mixed intellectual, student and bohemian population ensures there are enough theatre, music and film options to keep you occupied all year round. For detailed information, including all the best music and night-club venues, see *The List* entertainments magazine (also online at www.list.co.uk) or look for a copy of the city's daily, *the Edinburgh Evening News*.

MUSIC

The Edinburgh Festival (see page 60) attracts many world-class performers in opera, chamber and symphonic music, and jazz and pop, though it's possible to catch good performances throughout the rest of the year, with many pubs holding regular sessions in Scottish traditional music (see box).

There's also a vibrant local jazz scene; check *The List* for the latest events or head to **The Jam House** (5 Queen Street; tel: 0131-220 2321; www.thejamhouse.com). Although the city does not have a resident symphony orchestra, the Royal Scottish National Orchestra and the Scottish Chamber Orchestra hold concerts at **Queen's Hall** (89 Clerk Street; tel: 0131-668 2019; www.thequeenshall.net) and **Usher Hall** (Grindlay Street; tel: 0131-228-1155; www.usherhall.co.uk); both venues also feature Scottish Opera performances. The Queen's Hall also hosts fun, informal ceilidhs – traditional Scottish dances accompanied by live music that appeal to a cross-section of locals and visitors of all ages. For Latin music, try bar/club **El Barrio** (www.elbarrio.co.uk) on Hanover Street.

The Royal Lyceum theatre hosts major productions.

THEATRE AND COMEDY

Edinburgh's **Festival Theatre** (Nicolson Street; tel: 0131-529 6000; www.capitaltheatres.com) is one of the largest theatres in Britain, with productions featuring visiting companies all year round, including performances by the Scottish Ballet, while the **Royal Lyceum** (30 Grindlay Street; tel: 0131-248 4848; www.lyceum.org.uk) is another major venue for plays, and the nearby **Traverse Theatre** (10 Cambridge Street; tel: 0131-228 1404; www.traverse.co.uk) has the best in avant-garde. The **Playhouse** (18–22 Greenside Place; tel: 0844-871 3014; www.playhousetheatre.com) tends to attract more mainstream musicals as well as concerts. For comedy all year round, **The Stand** (5 York Place; tel: 0131-558 7272; www.thestand.co.uk) is one of the UK's top venues with great comics every night of the week.

FILM

With one of Europe's largest film festivals taking place in June (see page 61), it's no wonder that Edinburgh offers a great choice of cinemas. Some of the best city cinemas are the **Cameo** (38 Home Street, Tollcross; tel: 0871-902 5723; www.picturehouses.co.uk), which features the latest art house and some mainstream flicks; the **Filmhouse** (88 Lothian Road; tel: 0131-228 2688; www.filmhousecinema.com), screening arts and old-time movies; and the **Vue Omni Centre** (Greenside Place; tel: 0345-308 4620; www.myvue.com), a modern multiplex with the latest releases on the east end of Princes Street.

Street performances abound during the Fringe Festival.

Best Traditional Pubs

Old Town and Around

The Bow Bar
80 West Bow; tel: 0131-226 7667; www.thebowbar.co.uk.
Eight real ales and 290 malts make this place a connoisseur's heaven.

Deacon Brodie's Tavern
435 Lawnmarket (Royal Mile); tel: 0131-225 6531.
A traditional Old Town Scottish bar named after the inspiration for *Jekyll and Hyde*. Prices are undoubtedly aimed at passing tourists, but it's still a great spot for an evening drink.

The Last Drop
74 Grassmarket; tel: 0131-225 4851.
A lively traditional establishment with low ceilings and low lighting. The name is a reference to the gallows that used to stand in the square.

Royal Oak
1 Infirmary Street (off South Bridge); tel: 0131-557 2976; www.royal-oak-folk.com.
Excellent spot for traditional folk music, played nightly until around 2am. If it's too rowdy in the main pub, downstairs tends to be quieter, although it gets pretty packed when it hosts the Wee Folk Club on Sundays at 8.30pm.

Sandy Bells
25 Forrest Road; tel: 0131-225 2751; www.sandybells.co.uk.
Wonderful friendly pub with live Scottish folk music – with a few other influences – every night. It's perennially popular, and half the fun is squeezing in. There is a great choice of ales on offer.

New Town and Beyond

The Abbotsford
3 Rose Street; tel: 0131-225 5276; www.theabbotsford.com.
This island bar with Victorian decor is a former haunt of Edinburgh's literati.

The Bailie Bar
2 St Stephen St; tel: 0131-225 4673; www.thebailiebar.com.
Cosy bar with great choice of ales and a local, friendly atmosphere.

Barony Bar
81 Broughton Street; tel: 0131-556 9251; www.thebarony.co.uk.
A lovely Sunday afternoon venue for reading the papers in the window seat or admiring the Victorian tiles.

The Café Royal Circle Bar
19 West Register Street; tel: 0131-556 1884.
A fine Victorian tiled bar near Princes Street attracting a varied clientele.

Teuchters Landing
1 Dock Place; tel: 0131-554 7427; www.teuchtersbar.co.uk.
Waterfront setting in Leith with extensive wine list as well as traditional ales.

The Castle in the morning light.

Tour 1

Old Town and Edinburgh Castle

This walk of the heart of the old city is just over 1.5 miles (2km), so you can easily do it in half a day, but, if you wish to spend an hour or two at each sight, this is a full day's walk

Edinburgh's most important historical sight and the centre of the city's tourism, the Castle is built on a dramatic piece of volcanic rock that survived the last Ice Age and protected a ridge of rock behind it from advancing glaciers. The resulting 'crag and tail' created a site for a well-protected town on raised ground between two valleys and beneath the towering fortress. The 'tail' leading down from the Castle supports the Royal Mile, so called because it runs the length of it, for 1 mile and 106yds (1.9km) down to the Palace of Holyroodhouse

The route begins at the historic Grassmarket, lurking below the south-facing drop of the castle rock, before leading up to George IV Bridge – one of many bridges crossing the valleys up to the Castle 'tail' – and now lined with tall buildings. Taking in one of Britain's most impressive cityscapes from Greyfriars churchyard, the route continues to the upper reaches of the Royal Mile itself, providing a deep history, in-

Highlights

- Grassmarket
- Greyfriars Tolbooth and Highland Kirk
- Royal Mile
- Writers' Museum
- Camera Obscura
- Scotch Whisky Experience
- Edinburgh Castle

Bagpiper on the Royal Mile.

West Bow Wizard

Victoria Street replaced the upper West Bow, which had zig-zagged steeply up to the Lawnmarket, causing consternation to those trying to haul goods to market. It is said to be haunted by a galloping headless charger ridden by a 17th-century resident, Major Weir, the 'Wizard of the West Bow', who was executed after confessing to a string of depravities.

triguing sights and fascinating range of museums. It ends with a tour of Edinburgh Castle, including a visit to the city's oldest building, St Margaret's Chapel.

GRASSMARKET

The cobbled **Grassmarket** ❶ has long since shaken off its down-at-heel reputation and now houses hotels, great pubs, cafés and restaurants, which in summer offer refreshments alfresco. Most of the tall tenements here were built in the 19th century, though a few older buildings survive, such as the atmospheric White Hart Inn, and at the east end close to Victoria Street, an early 17th-century stone house, constructed when most of Edinburgh was still built of wood. Nearby is one of the old wells sunk to supply Edinburgh with its first clean water in the late 17th century. Long ago the monks of the Greyfriars Franciscan convent held cattle sales here, but the Grassmarket is better known as the location of the public gallows where executions took place until the 18th century, often providing entertainment for the jeering mob.

The **Covenanters' Memorial**, where the gibbet stood, was created in 1937 and recalls the many martyrs who died alongside common criminals. The hanging of religious dissenters peaked in the 1680s under Catholic James II, but the original Covenanters were signatories of the National Covenant of 1638, opposing imposition of the English form of Protestantism.

West Bow in the times of the infamous Major Weir.

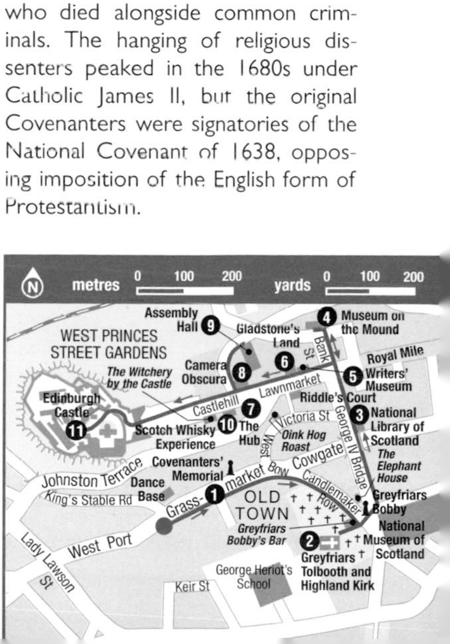

A much more modern addition to the Grassmarket has been Scotland's National Centre for Dance, **Dance Base** (www.dancebase.co.uk), located at the northwestern end of the square. With an exciting programme of workshops and classes for all ages alongside a full festival line-up of events, it's well worth finding out what's on.

West Bow

At **West Bow**, where the well stands, the wide Grassmarket splits into narrower roads. The **Cowgate** runs east along the lower edge of the Old Town, beneath the high arches of George IV Bridge and South Bridge. Once a route for cattle on their way to grazing on the Burgh Muir, the street became fashionable in the 16th century, yet following the building of the bridges above it in the 19th century its lower-level tenements had become immigrants' slum homes. Now it is liveliest after dark, with a number of bars and clubs. Curving uphill onto the bridge from West Bow on the north (castle) side is **Victoria Street**, noted for the individuality of its shops.

GREYFRIARS

At the southern side of the Cowgate, historic **Candlemaker Row** loops upwards, and contains the former **Hall of the Incorporation of Candlemakers**, built in 1722. Farmers would gather in the inns and taverns of this street, with the old, ram-

Beautiful stained glass inside Greyfriars Kirk.

Victoria Street is lined with a variety of shops.

The Grassmarket

The Grassmarket has some interesting small shops wedged between the restaurants and bars, and adjoining Victoria Street offers a wide range of curio shopping, with great unique clothing to be found at **Swish** (Nos. 22–4). For handmade Scottish woollies, try **Bill Baber** Knitwear Design (66 Grassmarket), while **Clarksons** of Edinburgh at 87 West Bow is an exclusive jewellers specialising in gold wedding rings. For kids and the young at heart, **Aha Ha Ha** (99 West Bow) is a joke shop and fancy dress venue that is something of an institution.

Greyfriars Tolbooth and Highland Kirk.

bling Greyfriars Bobby's Bar remaining at its summit. Opposite, on the corner of Candlemaker Row and George IV Bridge is the tiny statue of **Greyfriars Bobby**, the little Skye terrier who so faithfully visited his master's grave in Greyfriars churchyard each day from 1858 for 14 years, later to be immortalised the world over by Walt Disney.

Greyfriars Church

Perhaps the prettiest urban churchyard in all of Britain, the **Greyfriars Tolbooth and Highland Kirk** ❷ (www.greyfriarskirk.com) is situated behind the top of Candlemaker Row as it runs uphill from the Grassmarket, with many of the ornate tombs backing onto the houses on Candlemaker Row. Taking its name from the medieval Franciscan friary that stood on this spot, and with grand views up to the castle and well-kept gardens, the cemetery is an especially peaceful corner of the city, used as a favoured lunch spot on warm summer days. Among those buried in the churchyard are George Buchanan, tutor to James VI, the Earl of Morton, Regent of Scotland from 1572 to 1578, William Adam, the architect, Allan Ramsay, the poet, Duncan Ban Macintyre, the Gaelic poet, and William Smellie, who edited the *Encyclopaedia Britannica*. As you enter the grounds, you'll see a memorial to Greyfriars Bobby, laid to rest here in 1872, though his master, John Gray, is buried 40 yards/metres down the slope.

The church itself, though dating from 1620, was largely rebuilt in the 18th and 19th centuries on account of first an explosion – due to the council using the southern section for gunpowder storage – and second a devastating fire in 1845. Nonetheless tiny sections of the original structure remain, such as around the old entrance at its eastern end (now closed) and the old north door, still used as an entrance. Inside, the kirk is beautiful in its simplicity, and an interesting exhibition on its history reveals a copy of the original National Covenant. The Edinburgh home of the Highland Kirk, the church also offers a weekly service in Scottish Gaelic, 12.30pm Sundays.

Statue of Greyfriars Bobby, who was buried near to his master, just inside the entrance to the churchyard.

Jinglin' Geordie

The western side of Greyfriars Kirkyard is separated by the thick medieval **Flodden Wall**, which marks the old city boundaries, and beyond is **George Heriot's School**, named after the goldsmith, 'Jinglin' Geordie', who accompanied James VI to London. He became a moneylender and amassed a large fortune, which he left for the care and education of orphan boys – though these days the school is co-educational. Built in 1660 by William Wallace and William Ayton in Scottish Renaissance style, it was later improved by John and Robert Mylne.

To the south of the churchyard is **Covenanters' Prison**, where defenders of Scottish Presbyterianism were imprisoned under the English monarch Charles II in the 17th century (see box).

GEORGE IV BRIDGE

Opposite Greyfriars is the modern construction of the National Museum of Scotland, but heading northwards towards the Royal Mile you are walking along George IV Bridge, erected on nine arches by Thomas Hamilton in 1832 – though for most of its length you could be forgiven for thinking you are at ground level due to its terraced shops and high tenements above.

On the bridge's eastern side is the **National Library of Scotland** ❸ (www.nls.uk; Mon–Thu 9.30am–7pm, Fri–Sat until 5pm; also offers free internet usage), which has the right to request a free copy of every book published in the UK.

Just opposite the library, Victoria Street joins George IV Bridge, lined with a variety of small shops on its descent to the Grassmarket.

THE LAWNMARKET AREA

Further along the bridge you arrive at the ridge of the **Royal Mile**, the oldest thoroughfare in the city. The Lawnmarket section, up the hill from here, is where the produce of the surrounding land, as well as

The Covenanters

In 1638, hundreds of citizens, including many noblemen, flocked to the Greyfriars to sign the National Covenant. Its supporters, known as Covenanters, bitterly opposed the imposition of the English doctrines of Episcopacy (bishop-led Anglican church government) on Scotland, in favour of more traditionally Calvinist Presbyterianism. In 1679, 1,200 of them were imprisoned in cruel conditions for more than five months in the Covenanters' Prison, on the south side of Greyfriars Kirkyard, which can still be seen on a tour. Many of those who survived were subsequently transported to the colonies to be sold into slavery.

Lining up to sign the National Covenant at Greyfriars in 1638.

Drinking at the historic Deacon Brodie's Tavern, at 435 Lawnmarket.

wool and linen from 'landward' districts, was sold. A complex system of pends (vaulted passages), closes (entrances to tenement buildings) and wynds (alleyways) are found along the full length of the Royal Mile, often providing access to courtyards named after former inhabitants. **Brodie's Close**, on the left side going up the hill, recalls one of the city's more infamous sons, a town councillor and cabinet-maker by day, a burglar by night. His name is also immortalised at Deacon Brodie's Tavern, an historic pub on the corner of the Royal Mile and Bank Street, though more indirectly achieved permanent fame as the split-personality inspiration for Robert Louis Stevenson's *Strange Case of Dr Jekyll and Mr Hyde*.

Museum on the Mound

Some one hundred yards/metres to the north of George IV Bridge and the Royal Mile are the imposing towers of the former headquarters of the **Bank of Scotland**, built in 1806 and extended 60 years later. When the bank moved into new purpose-built premises outside the city in 2006, the building was turned into the **Museum on the Mound** ❹, located at the base of Bank Street (tel: 0131-243 5464; www.museumonthemound.com; Tue–Fri 10am–5pm, bank holiday Mon 1–5pm; free).

With a variety of displays focussed on the story of money and Scotland's role in its management, displays range from early bartering to the start of widespread home ownership in the 19th century, as well as temporary exhibitions on banknote design, forgery, vaults and robberies.

Back on the Lawnmarket, **Lady Stair's Close** on its northern side, named after its 18th-century owner, is where Burns lodged in 1786. These days it's home to the excellent **Writers' Museum** ❺ (tel: 0131-529 4901; www.edinburghmuseums.org.uk; daily 10am–5pm; free), containing relics belonging to Sir Walter Scott, Robert Burns and Robert Louis Stevenson, Scotland's best-known literary ambassadors. The displays on Stevenson are particularly revealing, following his early years in Edinburgh through to publication of his best-loved works, *Treasure Island* and *Kidnapped,* and finally to his relocation to the South Pacific in 1888. Photos, recorded readings and first editions all add to the atmosphere.

Outside the narrow 400-year-old building that houses the museum, a number of paving stones are set

The Writers' Museum.

into the attractive courtyard with quotations from the works of other famed Scottish writers.

Gladstone's Land gives some insight into 17th-century Edinburgh life and boasts some opulent interiors.

Gladstone's Land

The building located next door on the Royal Mile is **Gladstone's Land** 6 (tel: 0131-226 5856; www.nts.org.uk; mid-Mar–Dec 10am–5pm, tours only and by prior booking), the six-storey home of a prosperous 17th-century merchant. Its painted ceilings and authentic furnishings give an impression of life in Edinburgh's Old Town more than 300 years ago, and the house also boasts the original records of Scotland's disastrous attempt to colonise the South American Darien Gap in 1698, which almost bankrupted the country.

Riddle's Court across the road, dates from 1587 and became the residence of Bailie John McMorran, a wealthy merchant shot dead by a schoolboy while trying to quell a riot at the Royal High School. In 1598, a banquet was held here for James VI and his queen, Anne of Denmark, though these days the building is used for special events. Inside there is a painted ceiling and plasterwork

Outside The Hub, which offers festival information and ticket sales.

from the 16th and 17th centuries, while its external wooden staircase is typical of the period.

CASTLE HILL

On the far side of the mini-roundabout dividing the Lawnmarket from Castlehill, the top section of the Royal Mile, the former **Tolbooth St John's Church** has been transformed into **The Hub** ❼, Edinburgh's Festival Centre with a ticket booth and café (tel: 0131-473 2015; www.the-hub-edinburgh.com; booth: Mon–Sat 10am–5pm, extended hours during festival; café: see page 27). The 19th-century church was designed by James Gillespie Graham and Augustus Pugin and has a 240ft (73m) spire, the tallest in Edinburgh.

Ramsay Garden

A little higher on the right is the **Camera Obscura** ❽ (tel: 0131-226 3709; www.camera-obscura.co.uk; daily Apr–Jun and Sept–Oct 9.30am–8pm, July–Aug 9am–10pm, Nov–Mar 10am–7pm; under fives go free; see box), housed in the Outlook Tower, a tenement said to have once been occupied by the Laird o'Cockpen, a 17th-century lord provost, extended by the architect Sir Patrick Geddes in the 19th century. Geddes was also responsible for **Ramsay Garden**, a short diversion down steep, cobbled Ramsay Lane next to the tower. A delightful residential complex, it contains the former home of fine Scot-

From Prudence to Excess

The flamboyant edifice of the Bank of Scotland, on The Mound for 200 years, symbolised the triumph of the canny Scots' success in financial management, virtues of prudence and propriety, which made Edinburgh one of the largest financial centres in Europe. The collapse of the bank in 2008 amidst allegations of reckless investment, together with its bailout by government and the London-based Lloyds Group, dealt a serious blow to the Scottish self-image – despite the crisis being heavily linked to events overseas.

The Bank of Scotland building is now a museum about money.

tish poet Allan Ramsay (1686–1758) and his painter son, also Allan Ramsay (1713–84).

Follow the street around the corner for open scenic views over the New Town towards the Firth of Forth, and to see the **Assembly Hall** ❾, designed by William Playfair. Every May this is the meeting place of the General Assembly of the Church of Scotland, and a statue of the heavily bearded founder of Presbyterianism, John Knox, is to be found in the courtyard. For most of the year the building's **New College** is occupied by students of theology at Edinburgh University and is closed to the public, though events take place in the three performance spaces during the Festival.

Scotch Whisky Experience

Nearing the top of Castlehill is the entertaining **Scotch Whisky Experience** ❿ (tel: 0131-220 0441; www.scotchwhiskyexperience.co.uk; daily Sept–Mar 10am–5pm, Apr–Aug until 6pm). A tour lasting about an hour guides you through whisky's history, with a barrel ride through whisky production and advice on appreciation of both blends and single malts, with a free dram thrown in. The museum shop claims to offer the World's Largest Scotch Whisky Collection, and it's not hard to believe. Across the road is the **Tartan Weaving Mill and Exhibition** (daily 9am–5.30pm; free) a large shop and exhibition where visitors can see weaving on a working loom and have their photos taken dressed in Highland garb.

The old building next to the Whisky Experience dates back to 1630 and is named Canonball House after the iron shot embedded in the west gable; according to

The Camera Obscura has a regular show of live panoramic and close-up images of the city.

Kids will enjoy staring at the hypnotic holograms.

World of Illusions

Perfect for entertaining children, the Camera Obscura provides live images of the surrounding city through a periscope, and a series of mirrors allows you to play with images of buildings and people. A mesmerising exhibition of eye-deceiving holograms and 3D light-twisting illusions adds to the appeal.

Learn all about whisky production at the fascinating Scotch Whisky Experience.

legend, this was fired from the castle ramparts during the 1745 Jacobite siege, when Bonnie Prince Charlie occupied Holyroodhouse. Nearby, in front of the castle esplanade, a fountain and plaque mark the spot where witches and warlocks were burned from the 16th to 18th centuries, after being half drowned in the Nor' Loch – the lake long since replaced by Princes Street Gardens and Waverley Station.

EDINBURGH CASTLE

Perched high on an extinct volcanic outcrop and dominating the skyline is **Edinburgh Castle** ⑪ (tel: 0131-225 9846; www.edinburghcastle.gov.uk; open daily Apr–Sept: 9.30am–6pm; Oct–Mar: 9.30am–5pm; steward guided tours and audio tours). On the esplanade each August is held the Edinburgh Military Tattoo, one of the great spectacles of the festival season.

One of the best-known features of Edinburgh Castle is the **One O'Clock Gun**, fired from the ramparts daily at 1pm except Sunday. Tradition dictates that true natives of Edinburgh, wherever they are in the world, stop and look at their watches at one o'clock. You'll find the gun on Mills Mount Battery beside the self-service **Redcoat Café**.

View of Castle Hill, the top section of the Royal Mile, from the Outlook Tower, which houses the Camera Obscura.

On crossing the drawbridge leading to the Castle, notice the statues of King Robert the Bruce and Sir William Wallace, heroes in battles against the English.

Some History

Though recent excavations have unearthed evidence of Iron-Age and Dark-Age forts here – suggesting the site was occupied in 850 BC – by AD 600 it was occupied by the post-Roman Gododdin tribe, who named it Dun Edein (still the name for Edinburgh in Scots Gaelic), before it fell to Northumbrian Angles in 638.

The present structure dates from around 1,000 years ago, when 11th-century king Malcolm III and his Saxon queen, Margaret, lived at Edinburgh Castle, after which it became a frequent retreat for the Scottish monarchy. Withstanding over five centuries of sieges and occupations, most involving the English, it is remarkable that so much of it has survived. From the 12th century, every occupant has modified or added to it, so that today it is a rich architectural mix of palace, fortress, barracks, chapel and war memorial. Today, the Governor of Edinburgh Castle is the commanding officer of the British Army in Scotland, who is ceremonially called the 'keeper of the keys', guarding the castle for the Queen.

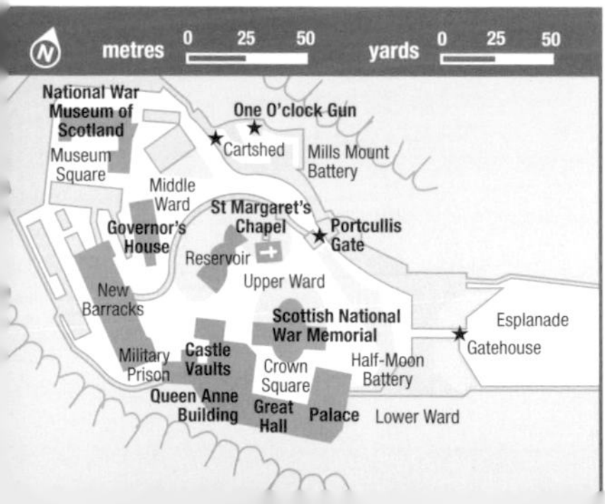

Castle Tour

As you enter across the modern **drawbridge** and **gatehouse**, ahead is the great parapet of the **Half-Moon Battery**, built by Regent Morton in 1574 on the ruins of the 14th-century David's Tower. The **Portcullis Gate** beyond dates from the same period.

Heading upwards to the castle's summit at **Crown Square**, the

18th-century **Queen Anne Building** is located next to the **Scottish National War Memorial**, designed in 1927 by Sir Robert Lorimer and now containing the names of the dead of the two world wars. On the south side of the square the **Great Hall** dates from the 16th century and is still used today for ceremonial purposes, dramatised by the ornate carved hammerbeam ceiling. Also in the square is the 15th-century **Palace**, containing among its royal apartments **Queen Mary's Room**, where in 1566 Mary, Queen of Scots gave birth to James VI of Scotland (who became James I of England).

The **Crown Room** on the first floor displays the Scottish crown jewels, the **Honours of Scotland**. The Scottish crown is one of the oldest in Europe, said to date from the reign of Robert I in the 14th century, but with arches from an older crown. The sceptre was a gift from Pope Alexander VI to King James IV in 1494, and the sword of state was given to the same king by Pope Julius II.

When Oliver Cromwell occupied Scotland in 1651, the Scottish regalia were removed for safekeeping, laying

The Literary Pub Crawl

One of Edinburgh's most popular tours is the Edinburgh Literary Pub Tour (May–Sept daily, Apr, Oct Thu–Sun, Jan–Mar Fri, Sun, Nov–Dec Fri; all tours start at 7.30pm outside The Beehive Inn in Grassmarket; 0131-226 6665; www.edinburghliterarypubtour.co.uk). A pair of droll actors, experts in witty rapport, whisk you around the Old Town via pubs, closes and courtyards, spanning more than 300 years of literature from James Boswell to Ian Rankin. Along the way you'll encounter the boozy haunts of the likes of Robert Burns and Sir Walter Scott, plus more modern associations such as J.K. Rowling.

The Elephant House claims to be the 'birthplace' of Harry Potter.

Sweeping view of the West End from Edinburgh Castle.

buried in a churchyard until the Restoration. It was not until 1822, when King George IV announced that he was to visit his Scottish subjects that the honours were put on display. Also in the Crown Room is the **Stone of Destiny** (or Stone of Scone), the traditional coronation seat of Scottish monarchs, which was stolen by English King Edward I around 700 years ago, and not returned until 1996.

St Margaret's Chapel

Behind the War Memorial, on the castle's northern side, is Edinburgh's oldest building, the 12th-century **St Margaret's Chapel**, said to have been built by David I for his mother, Queen Margaret, who died in 1093; the stained-glass windows, however – one of which features a likeness of Margaret – were inserted into the existing openings in the 1920s. On the ramparts in front of the chapel is **Mons Meg**, a 6-tonne (6,000kg) cannon allegedly employed at the siege of Norham in the 15th century.

On the left of the **New Barracks** (1796), which houses one of two regimental museums, on the lower-west side of the castle are the **Military Prison** and **Castle Vaults**, where prisoners of war were held in the 18th and 19th centuries. To the right, the former Ordnance Storehouse and Hospital is now the **National War Museum of Scotland**, with engaging displays on the nation's military history and the life of the soldier from Culloden to Iraq.

The **Governor's House** in the Middle Ward was built in 1742 as the

Stained glass in St Margaret's Chapel.

Castle Governor's official residence, and it now houses the Army Officers' Mess with magnificent views over the city from the Jacobite Dining Room.

Above the Castle entrance is the coat of arms of Regent Morton, who rebuilt it after the Lang siege (1571–73).

Eating Out

Amber Restaurant
The Scotch Whisky Experience, 354 Castlehill, Royal Mile; tel: 0131-477 8477; www.amber-restaurant.co.uk; daily from 10am, last orders 7.30pm Sun–Thu, 9pm Fri–Sat.
For lunch expect a wide range including salads and sandwiches, and even Scottish tapas. Main meals and desserts feature too. For dinner, first-rate service is accompanied by an innovative menu including fillet of Shetland salmon with crab fritters, steak with whisky cream sauce and good veggie options. ££

Café Hub
Castlehill; tel: 0131-473 2067; daily 10am–5pm.
Attractive café set in a historic church and festival booking centre very close to the Castle. The inventive sandwiches, salads and hot lunches are tasty and good value. Sunday brunch and afternoon tea is also available. ££

The Elephant House
21 George IV Bridge; tel: 0131-220 5355; www.elephanthouse.biz; Mon–Thu 8am–10pm, Fri 8am–11pm, Sat 9am–11pm, Sun 9am–10pm.
With views of the Castle from a room at the rear, this café offers a superb and good-value Scottish breakfast, alongside coffees, cakes and light lunches. It gets busy at lunch. £

Greyfriars Bobby's Bar
30–34 Candlemaker Row; tel: 0131-225 8328; food served noon–10pm.
This popular pub serves decent and good-value food. Soups, salads, sandwiches, sharing platters and mains such as steak and ale pie or haggis, neeps and tatties are a bargain. ££

Oink Hog Roast
34 Victoria Street; tel: 07771-968 233, www.oinkhogroast.co.uk; daily 11am–5pm.
This place is more of a take-away experience than a sit-down meal but it's a Grassmarket favourite. Mouthwatering roast pork rolls with crackling are served from the huge hog roasted each day. £

Spirit of Thai
44 Grindlay Street; tel: 0131-228 9333; www.spiritofthai.com; Tue–Sun lunch and dinner.
Located by the Lyceum Theatre, a few minutes' walk west of the Grassmarket, this attractive and friendly restaurant serves really good Thai food with Scottish ingredients, including sirloin steak with roasted rice and chilli sauce or seabass with black mushrooms and lemongrass. ££

The Witchery by the Castle
Castlehill, Royal Mile; tel: 0131-225 5613; www.thewitchery.com; daily lunch and dinner.
This atmospheric venue offers a theatrical candlelit experience featuring traditional/new-wave Scottish cuisine such as roast Cairngorm venison with bramble jus or Scottish oysters and langoustines. Simplified lunch menu at half the price. £££

The Heart of Midlothian outside St Giles' Cathedral.

Tour 2

Royal Mile and Scottish Parliament

At 1 mile (1.6km), this route covers the middle and lower sections of the Royal Mile, passing museums and the Scottish Parliament building, and can take up to a whole day

Much of Scotland's turbulent history was enacted along the Royal Mile, and you're never more than a few metres from a historical sight, place of gruesome intrigue or statue revealing the fascinating stories of past notable residents. Tour 1 covered the Castle Hill and the Lawnmarket sections of the Mile, while this one progresses down the **High Street** and **Canongate**, with a short diversion towards Waverley train station to visit the child-friendly Edinburgh Dungeon.

The top of the High Street is dominated by Parliament Square and multi-faceted St Giles' Cathedral, dating from as far back as the 12th century. Lower down, the best opportunity to bring the city's history to life for all ages is the excellent Scottish Storytelling Centre, while further antique closes, museums and a royal church all add to an en-

Highlights

- St Giles' Cathedral
- The Real Mary King's Close
- Edinburgh Dungeon
- Museum of Childhood
- John Knox House and Scottish Storytelling Centre
- Canongate Tolbooth and Kirk
- Scottish Parliament

Side Steps

Off the Royal Mile, it is well worth exploring some of the closes, or narrow passageways, which retain centuries-old features. One example, Advocate's Close, dating back to around 1544 has undergone regeneration, winning architectural awards, including Best Building in Scotland 2014, for its blend of the old and the new. It features apartments and offices, together with the Devil's Advocate bar set in a Victorian pump house.

Entering Advocate's Close.

thralling historical atmosphere. The modern Scottish Parliament at the base of the Mile offers a remarkable contrast – though not a conflicting style – and is certainly worth visiting as an illustration of the city's courageous approach to new architecture.

PARLIAMENT SQUARE

Surrounding St Giles' Cathedral, the Church of Scotland's principal kirk, **Parliament Square** fronts onto Parliament Hall, where the old Scottish parliament met until the 1707 Act of Union brought together Scotland and England. Essentially the central square of Edinburgh, this is where ceremonial events occasionally take place and where most of the city's many walking tours begin.

Immediately across the High Street, through arches which once contained shop booths, are the grand, neoclassical **City Chambers** (law courts), designed by John Adam in the mid-18th century, though taken over by the Town Council in 1811 having formerly been used as Royal Exchange offices. A statue by Sir John Steell, of Alexander the Great restraining his horse, Bucephalus, stands in the forecourt.

Heart of Midlothian

On the pavement in front of the west door of the St Giles' Cathedral is the **Heart of Midlothian**, a heart-shape worked into the cobbles where originally stood the Old (1438) and New Tolbooths, law courts, and lat-

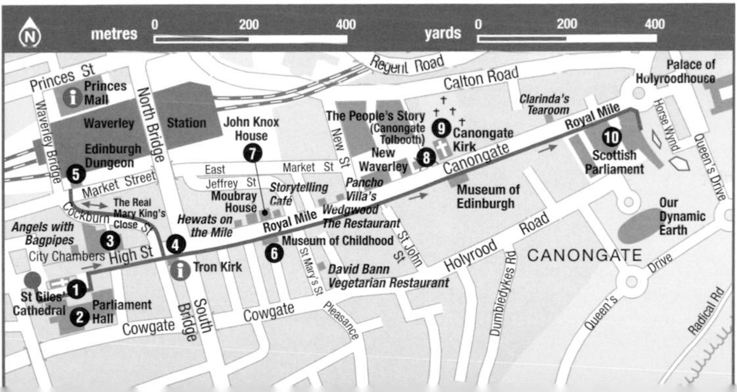

St Giles' Cathedral framed by a modern statue of David Hume.

terly the town jail and place of execution. As a consequence, the cobbled heart is traditionally spat upon by passers-by to show their contempt. Famed body-snatcher William Burke was executed here in 1829, reputedly viewed from above by the writer Sir Walter Scott, whose celebrated novel *The Heart of Midlothian* drew on the rich history surrounding the square. Scott managed to acquire the original Tolbooth's gateway, door

The great Gothic church with its distinctive crown-shaped steeple.

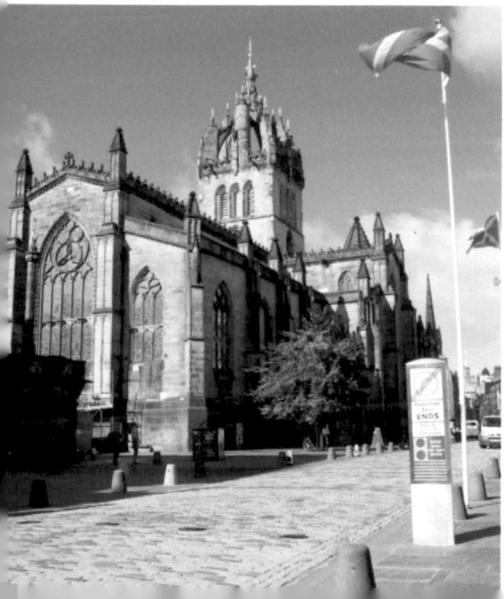

and padlock when it was demolished in 1817, using them at Abbotsford, the house he built for himself in the Borders (the area of southern Scotland adjoining England). Today, brass plates jutting into the road mark the outline of the original building, and a further brass plaque on the wall nearby tributes the last execution to take place – that of George Bryce, the infamous *Ratho Murderer*.

Close by are two statues, the first of the 5th Duke of Buccleuch, Lord President of the Council in 1846 – who built the harbour at Granton – and across the road, classically robed David Hume, the 18th-century atheist philosopher.

High Kirk of St Giles

St Giles' Cathedral ❶ (www.stgilescathedral.org.uk; Apr–Oct Mon–Fri 9am–7pm, Sat 9am–5pm, Sun 1–5pm, Nov–Mar Mon–Sat 9am–5pm, Sun 1–5pm; free) comprises architecture from the reign of Norman king Alexander I (1107–24), though the crown of St Giles' was added in the 16th century and the spire, supported by eight flying buttresses and topped with a golden weathercock, is from 1567.

John Knox, the great Scottish reformer, became its first Protestant minister after the Reformation, and a modern statue of him stands close to the west door, with his grave reputedly located in what is now the modern car park. Charles I made St Giles' a cathedral in 1633 by appointing a bishop, but attempts to introduce a new English prayer book alien to Scottish Presbyterianism resulted in riots and the bishop's removal in 1638 – though the continuing conflict between the more puritanical Scots and their remote rulers contributed to the outbreak of the English Civil War. Bishops were reintroduced at

Most of the stained glass in St Giles' dates to the mid- to late 19th century.

the Restoration in 1660, when Jenny Geddes, a local housewife, is said to have thrown her folding-stool at the preacher in St Giles', but they were again ejected 18 years later, and the cathedral reverted to its proper title of High Kirk.

The cathedral's interior has beautiful 19th-century stained glass, splendid memorials and a fine organ, designed by Rieger Orgelbau. The West Window is in memory of the poet Robert Burns, the Montrose and Argyll windows bear the arms of the Covenanters, and the windows in the Moray Aisle depict the funeral of the Regent Moray (Mary, Queen of Scots' illegitimate half-brother who was assassinated in Linlithgow).

Set on one side of the cathedral, the **Thistle Chapel**, designed by Sir Robert Lorimer in 1909, remains probably the most ornate post-medieval building in Scotland. The greatest Scottish public honour is to be made a Knight of the Thistle – the equivalent of England's Order of the Garter – and at any one time there are no more than 16 holders, all of whom

Spooky tours are plentiful.

Tours of the Underworld

You'd be hard pushed to find a city with more gruesome historical intrigue that Edinburgh. Though it gave birth to *Jekyll and Hyde* – which subsequently became a term in the English lexicon – the two-faced character is often applied to the city itself, with a darker side hidden behind a respectable exterior. With graveyard bodysnatching, public hangings of religious dissenters, plague-ridden cellars, and local authors who indulge macabre imaginations, numerous tours now take advantage of interest in all things sinister. Among the best operators are: **Mercat Tours** (daily; tel: 0131-225 5445; www.mercattours.com), who operate guided tours of the historic vaults in Blair Street below the bridges, graveyard ghost hunting and Royal Mile secrets; and **City of the Dead** (daily; tel: 0131-225 9044; www.cityofthedeadtours.com), who offer underground, graveyard and the Covenanters' Prison tours, among others. Tours last 1–1.5 hours.

The statue of the Duke of Buccleuch stands next to Parliament Hall.

have a dedicated chapel stall, each one carved in oak in elegant Gothic style with original heraldic stall plates enamelled by Phoebe Traquair.

Guided tours of the cathedral and rooftop are available, there's a shop situated in the Lower Aisle and a café located in the vaults, accessed from the south side.

Parliament Hall

From the west steps of St Giles', the **Signet Library** stands to the left, adjoining the **Advocates Library** and **Parliament Hall** ❷ (Mon–Fri 10am–4pm; access from No. 11; free). The Renaissance Parliament House had a facelift in the early 19th century (hence the false windows on the Georgian facade), and today it provides chambers for the judges of Scotland's Court of Session, advocates and barristers, who you can see pacing the Hall in their gowns and wigs. The Hall is 122ft (37m) long and 60ft (18m) high, with a 49ft (15m) wide hammerbeam ceiling of dark oak. The stained-glass south windows by Wilhelm von Kaulbach depict the inauguration of the College of Justice by James V.

The adjoining 19th-century **Signet Library** houses the books of the Society of Writers, Scotland's legal fraternity. Its beautiful interior boasts a classical ceiling that carries Thomas Stotland's 1821 painting of Apollo and the Muses. The salon of the upper library is often used for concerts and receptions.

In front of the building is the oldest equestrian statue in Britain, depicting (with some artistic licence) Charles II wearing the robes of a Roman emperor, and nearby another statue portraying James Braidwood, who started the world's first firefighting service in Edinburgh, before later carrying the idea to London.

See the city by bus.

Mercat Cross

On the east side of St Giles' is the **Mercat Cross**, from which proclamations are still made on state occa-

Royal Mile bagpiper.

sions. The original cross was virtually destroyed in the 18th century, but a small part of its shaft was incorporated into this 1885 replica. The cross marks a traditional trading place and – in keeping with the Royal Mile's somewhat macabre history – a former site of public tortures. The capital and the eight medallions proclaim the royal arms of Britain, Scotland, England and Ireland in company with the arms of Edinburgh, Leith, Canongate and Edinburgh University.

Not far down the street is the 2008 statue of Adam Smith, the pre-eminent Edinburgh author and founder of free-market economics. The statue features a bale of hay, which symbolises Smith's agrarian ideas, a nest, also signifying his beliefs, and the man himself is draped in philosopher's robes, somewhat obscuring his very public reputation as a benevolent eccentric and nightly sleepwalker.

The Real Mary King's Close

Underneath the City Chambers a warren of streets in what were the lower floors of original Old Town tenements have been uncovered, sloping down northwards from the Royal Mile ridge. **The Real Mary King's Close** ❸ (2 Warriston's Close; tel: 0131-225 0672; www.realmarykingsclose.com; daily Apr–Oct 10am–9pm, Nov–Mar Sun–Thu 10am–5pm, Fri–Sat 10am–9pm, although with some exceptions, so check before visiting) was sealed off in 1645 following an outbreak of plague in which hundreds died, but it has now been re-opened, bringing the past to life through a dramatic commentary.

You're essentially guided through a series of dank, dark cellars, some of which have models and furniture, while the well-trained guides offer a realistic, sometimes harrowing, but often amusing, account of the life

You'll find lots of tartan on the Royal Mile, but not always especially subtle.

The Shopping Mile

The Royal Mile is mostly given over to souvenirs and tartan, but running off it is Cockburn Street for alternative fashion and a selection of tourist kitsch, while for **highland dress and tartan** try Geoffrey Tailor Kiltmakers, 57–59 High Street and Tartan Weaving Mill, 555 Castlehill, or Hector Russell Kiltmaker, 137–141 High Street. For **whisky**, try Cadenhead Whisky Shop, 172 Canongate, or Royal Mile Whiskies, 379–381 High Street.

Fountain outside John Knox House.

of the poor in the Middle Ages. The close is believed to be haunted by plague victims, and there have allegedly been several sightings of a crying little girl in ragged clothes – one of a number of ghost stories that will appeal to older children.

THE HIGH STREET

At No. 180 High Street is the **Festival Fringe Society office** (tel: 0131-226 0000; www.edfringe.com; Jun–Aug, times vary), where tickets for the annual Festival Fringe shows can be purchased. A couple of buildings further on, at the junction with North and South Bridges, is the **Tron Kirk** ❹, built by John Mylne in 1637–48 and named after the 'tron' salt-weighing beam that once stood on the site. The kirk was reduced in size to make way for the South Bridge and Hunter Square 140 years later, and was also consumed by a fire in 1824 that destroyed the original steeple, along with a swathe of the south side of the High Street. It is owned by Edinburgh World Heritage and temporarily being used as a heritage centre, before its future is decided. Archaeologists have uncovered one of the city's oldest streets under the floor, which can be viewed.

The Museum of Childhood.

A short diversion from the High Street, down Cockburn Street towards Waverley Station (turn right along Market Street), will take you to another attraction located underneath the Old Town that brings to life the darker practices of olden times. The **Edinburgh Dungeon** ❺ (tel: 0131-240 1001; www.thedungeons.com; daily 10am–5pm, extended hours in summer, reduced weekday hours in winter; reduced tickets when booked in advance online) offers a range of gore-themed rides and live shows that older children will enjoy.

The colourful, welcoming Fringe Festival shop.

Museum of Childhood

Beyond the Tron Kirk, the High Street broadens and continues its downward slope towards Holyrood. On the same side is the **Museum of Childhood** ❻ (42 High Street; tel: 0131-529 4142; www.edinburghmuseums.org.uk; Mon, Thu–Sat 10am–5pm, Sun noon–5pm; free), which lays claim to being the world's first museum of its kind. With a significant collection of historical toys, dolls and books, it will probably appeal more to reminiscing adults than kids themselves, though the old train sets may strike a chord with some. There are temporary exhibitions and a programme of events, plus a tempting shop selling plenty of nostalgic toys and games.

Opposite the museum, in Chalmers Close, is Trinity Apse, the only surviving fragment of what was the finest collegiate church in Scotland, Trinity Church and Hospital. Founded in 1460, the building, which formerly housed the **Brass Rubbing Centre**, has fine vaulted ceilings and rare Scottish and medieval brasses. Exhibitions are occasionally held here, and the establishment is hired out for events.

Slightly lower down the High Street (on the southern side), **Tweeddale Court** was once the home of the First Marquis of Tweeddale, Chancellor of Scotland in 1692. One of the restored courtyard buildings houses the **Saltire Society**, a group that seeks to promote and preserve Scottish culture.

John Knox House and the Scottish Storytelling Centre

A few buildings further down you'll see the unmistakable timber-panelled shape of **John Knox House** ❼ jutting out into the road and now part of the same complex as the excellent **Scottish Storytelling Centre**

Down in the Dungeon

Playing up to the city's gruesome crimes and punishments, the Edinburgh Dungeon recreates a range of historical scenes including the *Grassmarket noose* and story of bodysnatchers *Burke and Hare* – there's also a mind-boggling collection of medieval torture instruments. The Street of Sorrows is home to Edinburgh's plague victims. The recommended age is 8 and over.

The Edinburgh Dungeon – not for the faint-hearted.

Story Wall

The Scottish Storytelling Centre is one of the city's best-kept children's secrets, with opportunities to learn and illustrate Scottish stories, whether of the traditional or JK Rowling variety. Events offer organised sessions for creative youngsters, where whole new stories can be invented from a plethora of ideas and pictures, as well as puppet shows and song and dance. The interactive Storywall of well-loved tales is extremely popular with children.

Inspiring ideas – let the storytelling begin...

(tel: 0131-556 9579; www.tracscotland.org/scottish-storytelling-centre; Mon–Sat 10am–6pm, Sun noon–6pm July–Aug only; free – note that there's a charge to enter John Knox House). The house itself dates back from around 1490 and contains relics associated with the Protestant reformer, though in fact it's doubtful he ever lived here – evidence instead suggests that he preached from the bow window. More accurately, it was the home of James Mossman, goldsmith to Mary, Queen of Scots, perhaps ironic given Knox's contempt for the Catholic Queen.

The Storytelling Centre is housed in a mix of modern and older adjacent buildings on the site of Netherbow Port, the original east gate to the city, destroyed in 1764. There's an exhibition space and the Netherbow Theatre, hosting dramatised story-shows, traditional musical events and workshops. The Storytelling Café, featuring good food and wine also hosts some evening events.

Next door to John Knox House (on the upper side) is **Moubray House**, restored by the Cockburn Society in 1910, and probably the oldest occupied dwelling in Edinburgh, recorded as far back as 1477. Daniel Defoe, author of *Robinson Crusoe*, edited the *Edinburgh Courant* from here in 1710.

THE CANONGATE

Close by, at the junction of Jeffrey and St Mary's streets, you cross into the **Canongate**, which was once a separate burgh (town). Today, brass cobblestones outline the location of the medieval gateway – the only indication that there was ever a divide here. On the left is the Adagio Aparthotel,

Canongate Tolbooth.

The Canon's Gait

While Edinburgh expanded by creeping down the hill from the Castle, the burgh of Canongate, or 'canon's road', developed separately under the auspices of Holyrood Abbey. Many Scots nobles had homes along the Canongate, and some fine 17th-century mansions survive. The two towns were separated by the Flodden Wall and Netherbow Port, and those living outside the boundary of Edinburgh were unprotected from attack.

The simple, light-filled interior of Canongate Kirk.

incorporating the original facade of the Sailor's Ark building and marking a spot where history combines seamlessly with cutting-edge architecture. Pedestrian access from the Royal Mile links to a vibrant public square behind that forms the centrepiece of the New Waverley development, which is bringing life back into a part of Edinburgh's Old Town that had become neglected. On completion the area will incorporate hotels, offices and residential units, together with retail and restaurant options.

The **Canongate Tolbooth**, readily recognisable by its distinctive clock tower overhanging the pavement, was built in 1591 for use as a courthouse, prison and centre of municipal affairs, but today finds itself home to **The People's Story** ❽ (tel: 0131-529 4057; www.edinburghmuseums.org.uk; daily 10am–5pm; free), a museum telling of ordinary citizens' lives over the past 200 years with sounds, sights and smells.

On the south side of the Canongate, **Moray House**, built in 1628, served as Oliver Cromwell's headquarters during a stay in Edinburgh. Rumour has it that the Marquess of Argyll watched from the balcony as Cromwell's rival Montrose went to his execution in 1650.

Next door, **Huntly House**, a fine example of a restored 16th-century mansion, now vividly adorned in yellow ochre and red, houses the city's principal museum of local history, the revamped **Museum of Edinburgh** (tel: 0131-529 4143; www.edinburghmuseums.org.uk; Mon, Thu–Sat 10am–5pm, Sun noon–5pm; free). The important and sometimes eccentric collection includes John Knox's spectacles, Greyfriars Bobby's collar and bowl and, most importantly, the

Moray House.

The debating chamber, where seating is arranged in a hemicycle.

original deerskin National Covenant, signed in 1638.

Canongate Kirk

Dominating the northern side of the street, **Canongate Kirk** ❾ was built to serve the congregation ousted from the Abbey Church of Holyrood in 1691, when the latter was converted into a Catholic chapel for the Knights of the Thistle by King James VII (James II of England) – the Queen now worships here when staying in Edinburgh.

Most people come to the attractive graveyard, however, to see the resting place of seminal economist Adam Smith, who wrote *The Wealth of Nations* – his grave is to be found in the left street-side corner. Others buried here include hymn writer Horatius Bonar and young poet Robert Fergusson (a statue of him adorns the pavement in front of the Kirk), who was so admired by Robert Burns that he erected a stone over Fergusson's unmarked grave.

Just below the churchyard is the little-known **Dunbar's Close Garden**, a charming small walled plot laid out in 17th-century style with gravel paths, stone seats and box hedges. The Canongate once featured many such small gardens, and in the 18th century a "physic plot" would have been the only source of medicinal plants. Below the garden is **Whitehorse Close**, an attractive courtyard of whitewashed houses dating from the 17th centu-

Plentiful during the festival season, street entertainers bring the city to life all year round.

-y. In the 18th century, stagecoaches travelling to London departed from the (now defunct) White Horse Inn.

SCOTTISH PARLIAMENT

As astonishing as it is impressive, the **Scottish Parliament** ⑩ (tel: 0131-348 5200; www.parliament.scot; Mon–Sat depending on parliamentary sessions, one-hour tours available, booking essential; free; café hours same as building) dominates the foot of the Royal Mile.

The vision of Catalan architect Enric Miralles, the design clearly draws on Gaudí's work in Barcelona, but also has a definite hint of Scotland's own Charles Rennie Mackintosh in its innovative use of curves and colour. A complex modern design – such as roofs in the shape of upturned boats – is combined with the historic surrounding setting of Holyrood, and the building certainly brings something refreshing and radical to Edinburgh's skyline. Miralles made sustainability a central element of the design across the site. The grass-covered rear of the structure appears to grow organically from the city's slopes below Arthur's Seat, while the interior also offers surprises at every turn.

Unlike in most parliaments, the semi-circular main chamber is designed to be a debating forum rather than a set of opposing sides, and whilst it is dominated overhead by a complex structure of beams, it does maintain intimacy. The members' of-

Savouring the Servants

At the northwest end of the new Parliament compound a much older building, Queensbury House, has been incorporated. It was built in 1681 and soon after sold to the First Duke of Queensferry, one of the chief promoters of the Treaty of Union between Scotland and England in 1707. His inbred son, Lord Drumlanrig, was found in the kitchen here eating a servant boy whom he had roasted on the spit, apparently having escaped his restraints while the rest of the household was witnessing the signing of the Union.

Inscription inlaid into stone at the gates of Queensbury House.

The Scottish Parliament building was Catalan architect Enric Miralles' final project and won the prestigious Stirling Prize in 2005.

fices at first come over as quirky with their curved windows and desk space, but they're deceivingly larger than they look. To truly feel the force of the work, you have to get inside and take the (hour-long) tour.

The Parliament finally opened in October 2004, though its cost had spiralled to more than £400 million – ten times the original estimate. In addition to the controversial design and a series of accusations over transparency, further intrigue was added when Miralles sadly died at the age of 45 in 2000, well before the building's delayed completion. Nonetheless, the design has since won a clutch of prestigious architectural awards.

Home Rule

The first elections to a Scottish parliament in nearly 300 years were held on 6 May 1999, after a referendum confirmed the people's wish to self-govern. This reflected a shift in Scottish public opinion since 1979, when the 'yes' vote had gained less than a third of the total electorate. Surveys reveal that most Scots now consider themselves Scottish first and foremost, and British as an afterthought – emphasised further in 2007 when after years of Labour Party control the Scottish National Party's Alex Salmond (advocating secession from the UK) was elected First Minister. The Parliament and Scottish Executive are based in Edinburgh, with responsibility for legislation and government in domestic matters, while

Admiring the final design model of the Scottish Parliament Building.

Scottish constituencies today continue to be represented in London as part of the UK. Devolution from England continues to be fiercely contended under the leadership of the current SNP leader, Nicola Sturgeon.

Eating Out

Angels with Bagpipes
343 High Street; tel: 0131-220 1111; www.angelswithbagpipes.co.uk; daily lunch and dinner.
Contemporary dining meets the Old Town at this restaurant opposite St Giles' Cathedral. Lit with winged angel candlesticks, the upper dining room is a delightful space. Head chef Fraser Smith brings innovative ideas to his traditional, locally sourced ingredients to great effect. £££

Clarinda's Tearoom
69 Canongate; tel: 0131-557 1888; daily 9am–4.30pm (Sat until 9pm, Sun from 10am).
A far better bet for a traditional tea than for breakfast, this Royal Mile stalwart serves local church-goers and tourists alike a great selection of cakes, teas and light lunches. £

David Bann Vegetarian Restaurant
56–58 St Mary's Street; tel: 0131-556 5888; www.davidbann.com; all day from noon (Sat–Sun 11am).
One of the best vegetarian restaurants in Scotland, in the heart of the Old Town. A stylish interior with an exciting international menu, including goats' cheese, tofu, aubergine and nut dishes with a variety of imaginative sauces. ££

Hewats on the Mile
123b High Street; tel: 0131-557 5732; www.hewatsedinburgh.com; Mon–Sat dinner, Fri–Sat lunch also.
Smart and cosy Scottish restaurant at the heart of the Royal Mile. The small but inviting menu features mains such as Aberdeen Angus with green peppercorn sauce and blackened fillet of halibut – though the tenderloin of boar with pork belly is known to be the dish of choice. £££

Pancho Villa's
240 Canongate; tel: 0131-557 4416; www.panchovillas.co.uk; daily lunch and dinner.
Mexican food served tapas-style has been on the menu at this Canongate restaurant for over 25 years. Owner Mayra Nuñez ensures the dishes are authentic. ££

St Giles' Cathedral Café
High Street; tel: 0131-225 5147; Mon–Sat 9am–5pm, Sun 11am–5pm.
Hidden away in the Cathedral Vaults and accessed from its southern side, this café is great for coffee or a light lunch in auspicious surroundings. Salads, pies and baked potatoes are the order of the day, with some fish dishes as well as excellent cakes. £

Storytelling Café
Scottish Storytelling Centre, 43 High Street; tel: 0131-558 1333; www.tracscotland.org/scottish-storytelling-centre; Mon–Sat 10am–6pm, Sun July–Aug 12.30–5pm.
Set within the excellent Scottish Storytelling Centre, this is a good place to stop for wholesome lunches, coffee and cakes. Good-quality seasonal produce is paramount. £

Wedgwood the Restaurant
267 Canongate; tel: 0131-558 8737; www.wedgwoodtherestaurant.co.uk; daily lunch and dinner.
Paul Wedgwood uses the best of ingredients to create fabulous dishes bursting with flavour. Inspired by his travels and innovative with his local foraging, his plates include delights such as roasted cod with caponata, white beans and chorizo. £££

Literary Edinburgh

Edinburgh has inspired far more than its fair share of literary greats. Both *Sherlock Holmes* and *Harry Potter* were created here, amongst a host of seminal books now hailed worldwide

While Edinburgh is a city of great beauty, scratch the surface and you will find something of a dark side, replete with tales of witchcraft, warfare, ghosts and death.

EDINBURGH'S DARK SIDE

Robert Louis Stevenson, who grew up in the New Town and studied at the university, based his *Strange Case of Dr Jekyll and Mr Hyde* (1886) upon on a famous local murderer, and many have extended this parable of the divided mind to the city itself, contrasting its Calvinistic gentility with a low-life criminal mind. The thin veil of middle-class respectability was torn off again in the 1990s by **Irvine Welsh**, whose dark-humoured novels about drug addiction drew on his experiences growing up in the city's notorious Muirhouse scheme. His book *Trainspotting* (1993) was turned into a successful film (1996), and also served to enhance the city's reputation as a hub of creativity. A sequel, *Trainspotting 2*, was released in 2017. Fans of crime fiction will also delight in **Ian Rankin's** *Inspector Rebus* novels, which use familiar settings from all over the city.

FOLKLORE

Contemporary tales aside, it was **Sir Walter Scott** (1771–1832) who

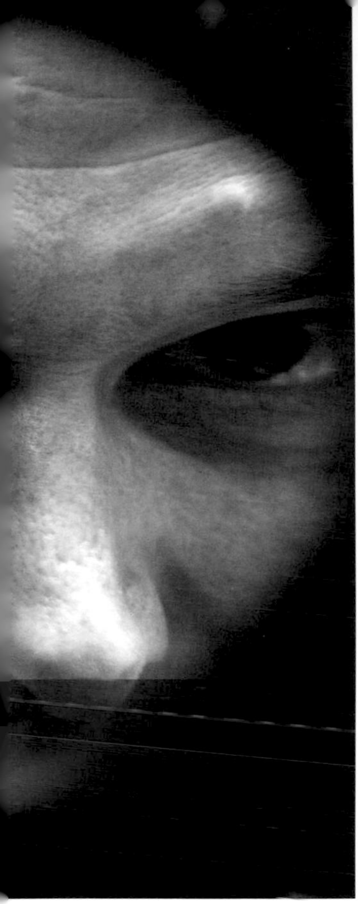

Ian Rankin, of Inspector Rebus fame.

really put Edinburgh on the literary map. Born into middle-class respectability, he met Scottish national bard **Robert Burns** (1759–96) in a New Town drawing room – an inspirational experience he would remember all his life. Eschewing a promising career in law, Scott ventured into the deepest folds of the countryside to record oral traditions, which he saved in prose and poem writing late at night in his home at 39 Castle Street. Through his masterpieces *The Border Minstrelsy, Marmion, The Lady of the Lake, Waverley* and *Ivanhoe*, many of Scotland's folk tales have been immortalised.

FROM SHERLOCK TO HARRY

It was at Edinburgh University that **Sir Arthur Conan Doyle** (1859–1930), who was born in a now demolished tenement block on Picardy Place, created the inscrutable detective Sherlock Holmes, basing him on one of his medical professors, Joseph Bell, who more can be learned about at **Surgeons' Hall Museums**. Robert Louis Stevenson (1850–94), a contemporary of Doyle at the university, also immortalised an aspect of his childhood through his famous work *Treasure Island* (1883), which was inspired by the pond in the gardens in front of his home. He didn't wish to have a monument erected in his memory – but you will find a child's garden where a flagstone carries his initials in Princes Street Gardens.

A friend of Doyle and Stevenson, **JM Barrie**, who was born in Kirriemuir, also studied at the university before penning his famous play *Peter Pan* (1901). Edinburgh has also produced **Muriel Spark**, best known for *The Prime of Miss Jean Brodie* (1961), set around the New Town Academy, while university professor **Alexander McCall-Smith** has achieved more recent fame with *The No.1 Ladies' Detective Agency* and his less-known but equally excellent series *44 Scotland Street*. Perhaps more than any other contemporary author, Edinburgh resident **JK Rowling** has achieved international stardom with the *Harry Potter* series, allegedly conceived in the Elephant House café on George IV Bridge in the Old Town.

A fun way to find out more on literary Edinburgh is on the **Literary Pub Crawl**, and memories and relics on Scott, Stevenson and Robert Burns are also held in the Writers' Museum off the Royal Mile.

The Abbey Church at the Palace of Holyroodhouse.

Tour 3

Palace of Holyroodhouse and Arthur's Seat

Holyrood Park, and its highest peak Arthur's Seat, offers the best views of Edinburgh. Combine it with a visit to the Palace of Holyroodhouse in an exciting 4-hour walk (2.5 miles/4km)

Beginning at the base of the Royal Mile, directly opposite the Scottish Parliament, the Palace of Holyroodhouse is the second major historical attraction after the Castle and one of the British monarchy's prized possessions, with a remarkably rich history stretching back to the 12th century. Most often connected to Mary, Queen of Scots and her son James VI, the palace has witnessed the full upheaval of relations between Scotland and England, with different periods occupied by both Oliver Cromwell and Bonnie Prince Charlie. Today, it makes for an enlightening tour, with a sumptuous interior accompanied with numerous anecdotes.

Highlights

- Palace of Holyroodhouse
- Our Dynamic Earth
- Arthur's Seat
- Duddingston Village and the Sheep Heid Inn

If you're walking with children, they may well appreciate the scientific exhibition 'Our Dynamic Earth', which delves into all things astronomical, though adults and children alike will love the climb up extinct volcano Arthur's Seat – a piece of the Highlands right there in the city. Finish the walk with a drink or bite to eat among the

Palace of Holyroodhouse.

neat terraces of Duddingston Village, where the Sheep Heid Inn serves good food and ales – a corner of the city pretty enough to inspire painter Sir Henry Raeburn.

HOLYROODHOUSE

The Queen's home when in Edinburgh, the **Palace of Holyroodhouse** ❶ (tel: 0131-556 5100; www.royalcollection.org.uk; daily Apr–Oct 9.30am–6pm, except during Queen's visits during May/June, Nov–Mar 9.30am–4.30pm) is amongst the most ancient of the residences still occupied by the British Royal family.

You can look around a great deal of the complex, which includes the main palace, remains of the 13th-century Abbey Church, the ornate palace gardens (there is a Garden History tour available), and the **Queen's Gallery**, situated by the western gate in front of the palace and featuring changing exhibits from the priceless Royal collection of classic paintings and jewellery. Monarchists will adore the Gallery shop, which contains royal paraphernalia, china and stationery. The Queen's personal apartments lie in the palace's south range and remain closed to the public; her residence is signified by the flying of the Union Jack over the palace as opposed to the red/yellow Scottish Lion Rampant flag at other times.

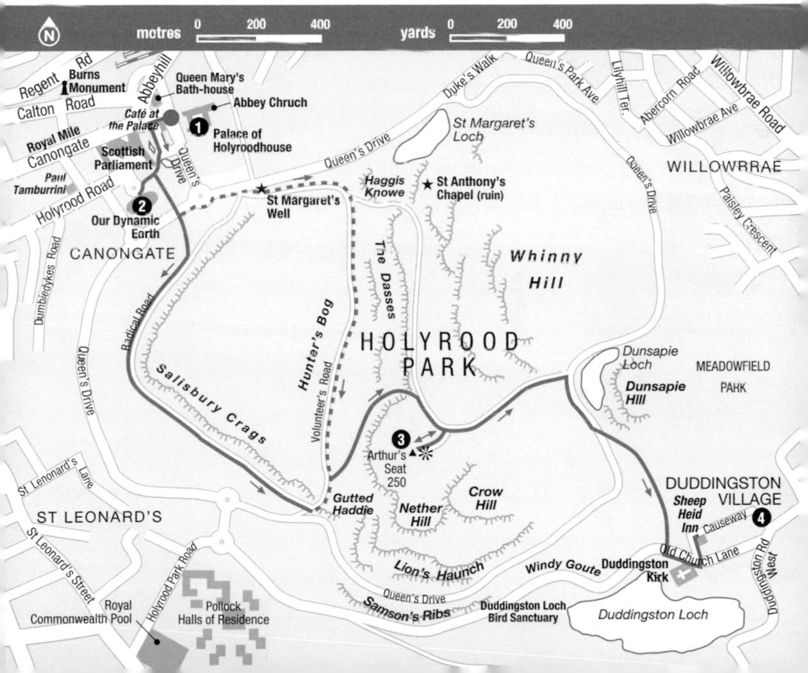

The palace began life as an Augustinian abbey and grew into a royal palace in the early 16th century to provide a more comfortable alternative to the Castle.

Holyroodhouse is closely associated with Mary, Queen of Scots, and the structure was transformed into something resembling the present royal palace layout during both her and her father's, King James V, 16th-century reigns. Its history goes back much further, however. Founded in 1128 by King David I as an abbey for Augustinian canons, the palace takes its name from a relic believed to have been a segment from Christ's cross (*rood* means cross).

Ornate lantern at the palace, topped with the royal crown.

All that remains of the original Holyroodhouse is the ruined nave of the **Abbey Church**, which served Edinburgh congregations and became a royal chapel when Charles I was crowned king here in 1633. Fifty years later it was destroyed by Orangemen who purged it of its Catholic ornamentation after the bloodless revolution of 1688; nonetheless, still to see here are the graves of several kings along its south aisle.

Just to the north of the palace on Abbeyhill stands **Queen Mary's Bath-house**, a quaintly shaped 16th-century bothy, which although carrying this name, offers no historical evidence to suggest that the Queen ever made use of it. Beside it are the northern gates of the Palace of Holyroodhouse and the Abbey Strand, which comprises two 16th-century houses, and now plays host to a Learning Centre.

The North and West Ranges

At the turn of the 16th century, part of the abbey compound was made into a royal residence for James IV and his consort Margaret Tudor (sister of

The evocative ruins of the 12th-century Abbey Church.

English King Henry VIII), west of the Abbey Church. Their son, James V, extended the building after 1528 by adding the tower-like northwestern corner, which today is the palace's most atmospheric section. The western range was completed when Mary, Queen of Scots, his daughter, took up residence with her second husband (and cousin), Lord Darnley.

Royal Rebellion and Decline

Despite the building's bloody history, Mary's son, James VI, made full use of it before he departed to London to become James I of England in 1603. He returned for one brief visit, and said in London: 'This I may say of Scotland, and may truly vaunt it; here I sit and govern it with my pen. I write and it is done, and by a Clerk of the Council I govern Scotland now, which others could not do by the sword.' With the absence of permanent royal residence, the palace suffered further indignation, when Oliver Cromwell bombarded it with fire in his campaign against James' grandson, English King Charles II. Despite Cromwell's victory against the royalists, Charles II was crowned King of Scots at Scone in 1651 after agreeing to the terms of the National Covenant – and it was he who truly established Holyrood as Scotland's royal residence within the modern British constitutional monarchy. Though he never lived there, he oversaw its reconstruction with a new facade and extravagant decoration.

Charles II lavishly furnished the drawing rooms and the state rooms, which have fine plasterwork ceilings, an idea clearly borrowed from his French contemporaries. The curious portraits in the long Picture Gallery are also well worth a good look at; supposedly Scottish monarchs, the 111 likenesses by Jacob de Witt ac-

Murder in the Palace

Mary's suite of rooms in the northwestern tower hold most interest, including original timber ceilings and the Queen's bedroom. Mary's secretary, David Rizzio, was notoriously murdered here in 1566 in an act of exceptional brutality, and a conspiracy in which Darnley was implicated. Justice was perhaps served when Darnley himself was murdered in the nearby residence of Kirk O'Field the following year.

Mary witnessed the savage murder of David Rizzio.

Learning about prehistoric creatures at Our Dynamic Earth.

tually all resemble Charles II, who seemingly commissioned them with the desire to display a clear line through the Stewart dynasty. In fact, more than 30 of the assembled faces probably never existed.

In 1745, Prince Charles Edward Stuart (Bonnie Prince Charlie) arrived from France, raised an army in the Highlands and occupied Holyrood for a short time before his victory at the Battle of Prestonpans, which was part of his campaign to win back the British throne for his father, the *de jure* James VIII (James III of England) – what became known as the Jacobite Rebellion. Though the 1707 Act of Union ensured that the Honours of Scotland – the Sword of State, Crown and Sceptre – remained bricked up within the castle, they were put on show in the Holyrood Palace state rooms during a levee for George IV in 1822, organised by celebrated Scots author Sir Walter Scott.

Throughout the 19th century, Queen Victoria started to use the palace regularly as a royal residence, something continued later by Elizabeth II.

OUR DYNAMIC EARTH

From the palace, cross the road towards the park and follow the path behind the parliament building to the hugely popular **Our Dynamic Earth** ❷ (tel: 0131-550 7800; www.dynamicearth.co.uk; daily Apr–Oct 10am–5.30pm, last entry 4pm, Jul–Aug until 6pm, last entry 4.30pm, Nov–Mar Wed–Sun 10am–5.30pm), which offers the ideal antidote to history and antiques-weary visitors. One of Scotland's biggest Millennium projects, the centre is housed in a futuristic marquee-like building with an impressive modern amphitheatre out in front: the paths that climb up to

Our Dynamic Earth

Near the eastern end of the Royal Mile, Our Dynamic Earth is an interactive exhibition that will keep children enthralled for hours. It tells the story of the planet through state-of-the-art earthscapes, including earthquakes, ice ages and tropical rainstorms, and you have the option to see, hear, feel and smell the planet as it was millions of years ago – ably aided by a 360° film narrated by Scottish actor David Tennant.

Yellow submarine display at Our Dynamic Earth.

Salisbury Crags.

the centre are lined with rocks from each geological period, accompanied with interesting illustrations and descriptions. Once inside, you encounter a kaleidoscope of movement and colour, bringing to life astronomical science. After viewing the interactive displays, you can watch a film projection onto a full dome exploring ideas such as infinity and the story behind the stars (see box).

HOLYROOD PARK

Walk to the rear of the Our Dynamic Earth building and you quickly enter the royal estate of **Holyrood Park** (ranger service tel: 0131-652 8150; all year), 640 acres (259 hectares) of Highland-style parkland encircled by a road, Queen's Drive, and dominated by the 820ft (250m) volcanic mini-mountain **Arthur's Seat** ❸ and a steep ridge of cliffs called **Salisbury Crags**. From some city angles, the mountain and crags resemble a sleeping lion, and it is hard not to be impressed by their phenomenal location; moorland and mountain entirely surrounded by urban sprawl, and which is also the favoured jogging route of Edinburgh's fitness buffs. A walk around the park or up to the summit is not to be missed if you're in Edinburgh for more than a couple of days, and it provides a great perspective on the surrounding city.

Theories abound as to the origins of the name Arthur's Seat – some draw parallels with the stories of King Arthur, others with defensive *archers*, and another still from a Strathclyde prince in the Dark Ages. Salisbury Crags is more straightforward however, drawing from the English commander who rested his troops here in the early 14th century. Arthur's Seat was formed by an extinct volcano from the Carboniferous period

There are various routes climbing up to the top of Arthur's Seat, some more arduous than others.

of 350 million years ago – similar to Edinburgh's Castle Rock – but was eroded later by glacial movements that exposed the basalt crags below, something that both perplexed and inspired early geologists.

A few hundred yards/metres east of Our Dynamic Earth are the 15th-century **St Margaret's Well** and, nearby, the former boating lake of St Margaret's Loch – named after Queen Margaret of Scotland, wife of the 11th-century Anglo-Saxon king Malcolm III, who was canonised by the pope 150 years after her death. Above the loch stand the ruins of **St Anthony's Chapel**, a medieval monastery.

Routes to Arthur's Seat

The most exciting route through the park is along a footpath beneath the upper cliffs of Salisbury Crags – known as the **Radical Road** because impoverished radical weavers under the direction of Sir Walter Scott built it in the 1820s. Most people know the path solely from its reference in the classic Edinburgh tongue-twister, however:

'Round and round the Radical Road
The Radical Rascal ran'

Though longer than the direct route up Arthur's Seat (30 mins), this is probably the most impressive section of pathway, offering an incredible perspective on the *crag and tail* of the castle rock. From the far end of the crags take the sharp uphill trail to ascend **Arthur's Seat**, following the path around the summit and approaching from the east. A slightly shorter alternative is to follow the Volunteer's Road path, which leads up from St Margaret's Well, and through the valley on the other side of Salisbury Crags. If you wish to climb the easiest route straight up to the summit, walk (or take a taxi) around Queen's Drive to the **Dunsapie Loch**, from where it's about a 20-minute walk to the summit.

On a clear day, a fine view can be had right across to Fife, over the Firth of Forth estuary. Wear good footwear (preferably walking boots), and make sure you're carrying enough water for the walk.

DUDDINGSTON

Descend Arthur's Seat to Queen's Drive at Dunsapie Loch, and then continue to descend south eastwards on the trail to well-preserved and very attractive **Duddingston Village** ❹ named after a 12th-century Norman knight called Dodin, who leased the land from the Abbot of Kelso. Arriving on cobbled Old Church Lane **Duddingston Kirk** dates from the

Stunning view of Arthur's Seat from Calton Hill.

Duddingston Loch.

12th century (though additions were made later) and it's a very picturesque spot on the banks of natural lake **Duddingston Loch** – where Sir Henry Raeburn set his famous portrait of the Rev. Robert Walker skating, now to be found at the Scottish National Gallery. The loch is a wildlife reserve, with protected reeds, herons and other waterfowl.

Make sure you stop at the village's famous pub, the **Sheep Heid Inn** (see box). It was named in the 16th century when James VI is said to have presented the owner with a silver snuff box decorated with a ram's head, though it may have opened up to two centuries earlier, making it one of Scotland's oldest pubs. If you wish to catch a bus from the city centre to here, No. 42 traverses George IV bridge before continuing down Forrest Road/Bristo Place and along Buccleuch Terrace.

Eating Out

Café at the Palace
Palace of Holyroodhouse; tel: 0131-652 3685; www.royalcollection.org.uk; daily 9.30am–6pm.
Coffees, teas, light lunches and wine are available at this tourist-oriented café next to the Queen's Gallery (accessible without ticket). The outdoor terrace makes for a relaxing spot before heading up Arthur's Seat. £

Paul Tamburrini
Macdonald Hotel, 81 Holyrood Rd; tel: 0344-879 9028; www.paultamburrini.co.uk; daily noon–9.30pm.
World-class chef Tamburrini exceeds expectations at this hotel restaurant with his French cooking coupled with the finest Scottish ingredients. £££

Sheep Heid Inn
43 The Causeway, Duddingston; tel: 0131-661 7974; www.thesheepheidedinburgh.co.uk; daily Mon–Thu 11am–11pm, Fri–Sat until midnight, Sun noon–11pm, food served 12.30–9.30pm.
Claiming to date back 'from at least 1360', the present pub was built in the early 1900s and is well worth the short trip – whether or not you decide to climb nearby Arthur's Seat. Some lighter bites feature at lunchtime, but there is a full and varied menu served all day with well-loved classics and some more innovative dishes. It's best to book in advance. ££

Statue of James Watt at the National Museum of Scotland.

Tour 4

South Side Museums and University

South of the Royal Mile lie the city's top historical museums, all worth half a day's visit. At the end of this 1.5 mile (2km) route the university district unveils some architectural gems

It is rare to find a number of superb museums in close proximity to each other, and in the National Museum and Surgeons' Hall, there's a variety here to suit pretty much any taste. If you'd like to know more about almost any aspect of Scottish history, from William Wallace and Nova Scotia to whisky or Scottish identity today, there is a detailed display here for you to see.

The route also takes in the more historic parts of the University of Edinburgh, dating from the turn of the 19th century. You may wish to end the tour at the Surgeons' Hall, a fascinating and unusual collection of objects, documents and art relating to all things medical, including insights into Arthur Conan Doyle's *Sherlock Holmes*. Alternatively, continue walking to Queen's Hall, or catch a bus to medieval Craigmillar Castle, a beautifully preserved 15th-century fortress. If visiting two or three museums, this route can take up a full day.

Highlights

- National Museum of Scotland
- Old College, University of Edinburgh
- Festival Theatre
- Surgeons' Hall Museums
- Craigmillar Castle

Enjoying the displays at the National Museum of Scotland.

NATIONAL MUSEUM OF SCOTLAND

The route begins at the corner of George IV Bridge and Chambers Street, right opposite Greyfriars Tolbooth and Highland Kirk (see page 17). Chambers Street dates from an 1860s improvement scheme, named after the Lord Provost of the time, William Chambers, who founded the publishing company that still bears his name and whose statue stands in the centre of the street. On the north side, the former Heriot Watt University building is now the **Sheriff Courthouse**, while opposite stands the modern, sandstone-clad part of the **National Museum of Scotland** ❶ (tel: 0300-123 6789; www.nms.ac.uk; daily 10am–5pm; themed guided tours available all day; free), a superb addition to the country's facilities, completed in 1998.

With six floors and an attractive rooftop terrace, the museum brings under one roof Scotland's most valuable national treasures and tells the country's history from earliest times to the present day. Geology, flora and fauna, religious struggles, shipbuilding as well as emigration and explorations of Scottish identity are all woven together through impressive narratives, while artefacts on display range from Pictish gravestones to the famous 12th-century Lewis ivory chesspieces,

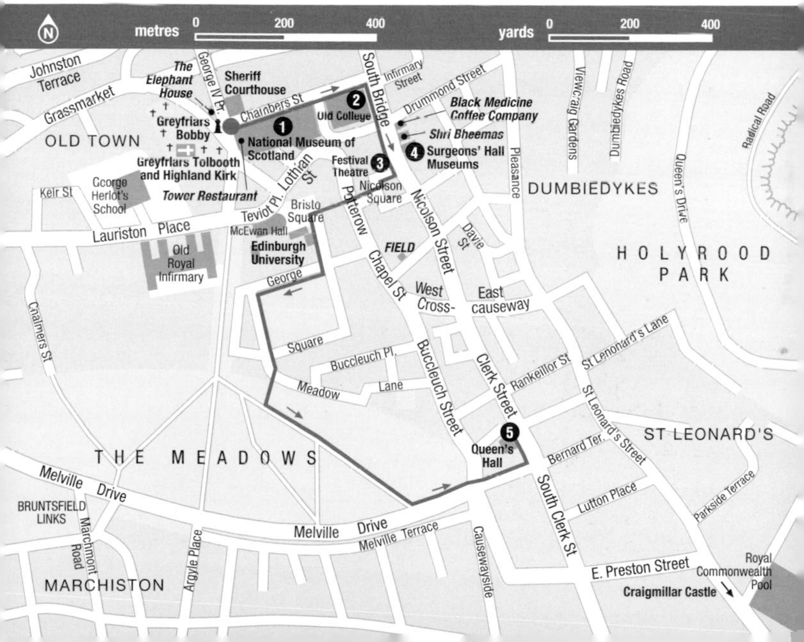

and silverware belonging to Charles Edward Stuart.

In 2011 the former Royal Museum, a magnificent 19th-century building designed by Francis Fowke on Chambers Street, became integrated with the National Museum following an extensive renovation, with access between the two buildings. It has a spectacular 270ft (82m) main hall roofed in glass, known as the Grand Gallery, which houses an eclectic collection of objects from ancient to modern. Ten new galleries opened in July 2016, six concentrating on science and technology and four dedicated to decorative art, design and fashion. Two further new galleries exploring Ancient Egypt and East Asia are due to open early in 2019.

Museums for Children

Edinburgh's best museums need not be a trauma if you're travelling with children. Accessibility for kids has been a major preoccupation for the curators of the National Museum, and it consequently offers a range of events especially aimed at children, enabling them to explore items from the collection. Start your visit in the Grand Gallery; don't miss the fabulous Millennium Clock and the fantastic Window on the World Gallery. On levels 4 and 5 you will find early trains (with an old engine) and cars, and displays on the natural world, including Adventure Planet offering children the chance to dress up to survive extreme environments. The science and technology galleries opened in 2016 add another dimension, with hand-on activities from the hot-air balloon challenge to the giant hamster wheel.

The Industry and Empire section of the National Museum of Scotland.

SOUTH BRIDGE

Follow Chambers Street onto the South Bridge. Two landmarks rise up from either end of the South Bridge the Tron Kirk and Old College. But you can only tell you're on a bridge by peering down at the Cowgate from above the single open archway. The buildings lining it are not on the bridge but flush with it, with basements in the valley below, and the other 18 arches of the South Bridge, built in 1785–88 to link the Old Town with the University, contain vaulted chambers once used as workshops and cellars.

Upon reaching the South Bridge you'll see the front of the University of Edinburgh's **Old College ❷**. The foundation stone was laid in 1789, but the building, to Robert Adam's design was only completed in 1834 by William Playfair, who was responsible for the interior design. The dome, surmounted by a small statue of a 'golden boy' carrying the torch of knowledge, was added in 1879.

The **Talbot Rice Gallery** (tel 0131-650 2210; call for opening times; free) in the college is a popu-

The National Museum's Grand Gallery.

lar venue for contemporary art exhibitions, and also has a small permanent collection of Old Masters and bronzes.

James VI granted a charter to found a college in Edinburgh in 1582, and the University was constructed on the site of Kirk o' Field, where pre-Reformation monasteries had been and where the Old College stands. Its present situation resulted from the vision of Lord Provost George Drummond, who masterminded improvements to the South Side as well as the creation of the New Town.

Opposite, Infirmary Street was where the original Royal Infirmary was sited from the early 18th century, and the University's renowned anatomical and medical schools grew in tandem with it – famed as the inspiration for Burke and Hare's bodysnatching activities (see box). Drummond Street is also lined with former University departments, attended variously by the luminary city writers JM Barrie (author of *Peter Pan*), Arthur Conan Doyle (*Sherlock Holmes*), and Robert Louis Stevenson *(Treasure Island)*, who has a plaque placed in his honour at the corner of South Bridge and Drummond Street.

Just around the corner, on South Bridge itself, a more recent (and tiny) plaque commemorates the birth of *Harry Potter*, whose author JK Rowling first conceived the character at The Elephant House café (see page 27). For more on literary Edinburgh, see page 42.

Festival Theatre

Beyond the South Bridge on Nicolson Street is the glass-fronted **Festival Theatre** ❸ (tel: 0131-529 6000;

The glass facade of the Festival Theatre.

Surgeons' Hall Museums.

www.capitaltheatres.com/festival), converted from the old Empire Theatre in 1994 by architects Law & Dunbar-Nasmith. Several theatres have occupied this site, including one that caught fire in 1811, causing the death on stage of the Great Lafayette, a celebrated illusionist. The present structure has almost 2,000 seats and a stage area larger than London's Royal Opera House.

Burke and Hare

The University's Anatomy Department achieved notoriety as well as recognition for its pioneering work in the early 19th century, when some professors purchased corpses for their dissection classes at the same time as recently buried coffins went missing from nearby graveyards. In 1828 William Burke and William Hare went a step further than the bodysnatchers by murdering the specimens they supplied to Dr Knox. Burke was hanged for his crimes in front of a crowd of 20,000, and his skin was flayed and sold. His skeleton is in the Anatomy Department's collection at Teviot Place.

Surgeons' Hall Museums

Opposite is the imposing neoclassical facade of the **Surgeons' Hall Museums** ❹ (tel: 0131-527 1711; www.museum.rcsed.ac.uk; daily 10am–5pm), again the work of William Playfair. Home to the Royal College of Surgeons of Edinburgh, the complex contains a series of fascinating exhibitions themed around surgery, anatomy and dentistry. Reopened in 2015, the Lister Project is a £4.3 million initiative enabling redisplay along with conservation of the building. It consists of the WOHL Pathology Museum (one of the largest collections in the world), the History of Surgery Museum and the Dental Collection, all covering the history of medicine from 1505 to the present day. It's not for the faint-hearted, with some gory items and vivid practices on show.

UNIVERSITY SQUARES

Turning west off Nicolson Street through Nicolson Square, the University buildings of **Bristo Square** and **George Square** beyond loom into view; both of these host a range of arts events through the summer. The former plaza is dominated by the huge Italian renaissance rotund **McEwan Hall**, used for graduation ceremonies and functions. In 2015 the University of Edinburgh invested £35 million on improvements to the McEwan Hall and the Bristo Square area. As part of the redevelopment, which was completed in July 2017, the artwork 'The Next Big Thing… is a Series of Little Things' by Susan Collis was installed – it takes the form of a number of bronze circular shapes that are like drips running across the square. Other noteworthy buildings here include the Reid Concert Hall, opened in 1859 and named after General John Reid, an army officer and musician who founded the Chair of Music at the University. At George Square, only the west and east sides remain intact, the rest having been bulldozed during 1960s redevelopment. The square was begun in the late 18th century by James Brown, who named it after his brother.

West of the University are the old buildings of the late 19th-century Royal Infirmary of Edinburgh (since moved to new buildings at Little France), originally the work of John and David Bryce though redeveloped into apartment buildings with contrasting (and brave) modern glass structures separating each of the old wards. Known as **Quartermile**, the development was completed in 2018.

Just south of the University and George Square are the **Meadows**, opened as a public park in 1860 and now a large green space with sports facilities and numerous festival events in August. A Burgh Loch before the 18th century, the Meadows were reclaimed during the Enlightenment by Thomas Hope of Rankeillour, the president of the Society of Improvers of the Knowledge of Agricul-

The Surgeons' Hall Museums cover Edinburgh's special contribution to surgical practice in modern times.

ture in Scotland. South of here is the student residential area of Marchiston, while east of the park on Clerk Street is the **Queen's Hall** ❺ (tel: 0131-668 2019; www.thequeenshall.net), a Georgian church designed by Robert Brown in 1823 and which hosts a range of classical concerts and other entertainment throughout the year.

CRAIGMILLAR CASTLE

A further diversion in the south of the city is **Craigmillar Castle** (tel: 0131-661 4445; www.historic-scotland.gov.uk; Apr–Sept daily 9.30am–5.30pm, Oct–Mar Sat–Wed 10am–4pm). Situated at the east side of Liberton beyond Duddingston (see page 50), it is easily reached by bus from the Queen's Hall (10 mins on Nos 30 or 49, alighting at the new Edinburgh Royal Infirmary, from where it's a ten-minute walk; by car take the Niddry exit from Cameron Toll roundabout on to Peffermill Road, then turn on to Craigmillar Castle Road).

This is one of Scotland's most impressive medieval ruins, an exceptionally well-preserved fortress with an L-plan tower dating from the late 15th century. Mary, Queen of Scots fled here in 1566 after the murder of David Rizzio, her private secretary, at Holyroodhouse. Later that year several Scottish noblemen are said to have met here to plot the murder of Lord Darnley, the Queen's husband (see page 47).

Craigmillar Castle was begun in the early 15th century by the Preston family, who had acquired the lands of Craigmillar in 1374. Sir Simon Preston was a staunch supporter of Mary, Queen of Scots and a member of her Privy Council.

The castle's highest point is the roof of the tower house, one of the oldest such towers in all of Scotland. From here you get stunning views in all directions. Edinburgh Castle lies on the skyline to the northwest, while to the north Salisbury Crags and Arthur's Seat command attention.

The surrounding grounds are a peaceful, relaxing space interspersed with trees, and unaffected by the rundown Craigmillar council housing estate that lies nearby.

Tables with a view at the Tower Restaurant.

The serene and well-preserved medieval ruins of Craigmillar Castle are picturesque at any time of year.

Eating Out

Black Medicine Coffee Company
2 Nicolson Street; tel: 0131-557 6269; www.blackmed.co.uk; Mon–Sat 8am–8pm, Sun from 9am.
Popular café for festival goers and university staff/students alike, with attractive wooden panelling, friendly staff and great coffees and cakes. £

Field
41 West Nicholson Street; tel: 0131-667 7010; www.fieldrestaurant.co.uk; Tue–Sat lunch and dinner.
Field is one for unpretentious, yet exciting, dining. Its chefs have worked in Michelin-starred restaurants and bring those exacting standards here. Dishes such as oxtail ragu with pepper pappardelle followed by roasted rabbit loin feature. Great set lunch menus are available too. ££

Rhubarb at Prestonfield House Hotel
Prestonfield Road; tel: 0131-225 1333; www.prestonfield.com; daily lunch and dinner.
Another of city restaurateur James Thomson's supreme range of eateries (which includes *The Witchery* and *The Tower*), Rhubarb features a superb and lavish ambience within this 17th-century mansion with views of Salisbury Crags and close to Craigmillar Castle. Classic Scottish/French cuisine and outstanding wine cellar. £££

Shri Bheema's
14a Nicolson Street; tel: 0131-558 7777; www.shribheemas.co.uk; daily lunch and dinner.
This award-winning chain, where customers are treated like one of the family, presents authentic South and North Indian dishes. Some old favourites mixed with new combinations of flavour appear on the menu and offer reasonably priced quality cuisine. ££

The Tower Restaurant
National Museum of Scotland, Chambers Street; tel: 0131-225 3003; www.tower-restaurant.com; daily 10am–12.30pm.
Edinburgh's first rooftop terrace restaurant showcases dishes such as Borders steak, Perthshire lamb rump and fine Scottish seafood. Affordable two-course lunch and pre-theatre menus at £19.95. £££

A City of Festivals

Edinburgh's August festivals are a cultural maelstrom. Famous comics are born, while new books, plays and music are showcased in front of ever-enthusiastic audiences

Most famous of all is the **Edinburgh Fringe**, which began life secondary in importance to the 'official' festival but has grown to become the main event in all but name with a line-up of over 700 companies spilling into every available performance space to present some 3,300 shows in over 50,400 performances in 300 venues. Its speciality is experimental theatre and stand-up comedy, and many of Britain's top comedians have used it as a launching pad. Alan Bennett, Peter Cook and Dudley Moore sealed their reputations here in 1960, followed by the debuts of Monty Python, Rowan Atkinson, Ben Elton, Stephen Fry and Hugh Laurie, and in later years anyone and everyone from Frank Skinner to Ricky Gervais, Bill Bailey to Sarah Millican. Pulling a decent-sized audience is the name of the game, and though bigger stars sell out early for their evening shows, you'll find many lower-key daytime performances often just as good. The best way to sort the decent from the drab is to look at the reviews in any English or Scottish newspaper.

The **Edinburgh International Festival** offers entertainment with a more high-culture label, such as large-scale theatre companies, opera and ballet in venues including the Edinburgh Festival Theatre, Queen's Hall

A Frenzy of Festivals

Edinburgh International Festival: www.eif.co.uk (most of Aug)
Edinburgh Festival Fringe: www.edfringe.com (most of Aug)
Edinburgh Military Tattoo: www.edintattoo.co.uk (most of Aug). Marching pipers and drummers mark this celebration of the military.
Edinburgh Art Festival: www.edinburghartfestival.com (end of July–end Aug)
Edinburgh International Book Festival: www.edbookfest.co.uk (second half of Aug)
Edinburgh International Jazz and Blues Festival: www.edinburghjazzfestival.com (one week in the second half of July)
Edinburgh International Film Festival: www.edfilmfest.org.uk (second half of June)
Edinburgh International Science Festival: www.sciencefestival.co.uk (April). Lectures and kids' events.
Imaginate Children's Festival: www.imaginate.org.uk (May/June). Theatre, dance and circus.
Edinburgh Mela: www.edinburghmela.co.uk (early Sept). A two-day celebration of Scottish Asian culture.

Blackwatch Piper at the Military Tattoo.

and Usher Hall. Dating from the end of World War II, the festival was the idea of Edinburgh's Lord Provost, Sir John Falconer, who came up with the concept of a celebration of the arts to play a role in the healing process between nations – as well as serving to re-establish Edinburgh as a European city of culture. With finance from the British Arts Council, the curtain went up on the first production in 1947. Its resounding success launched Edinburgh's worldwide reputation. The famous violinist Yehudi Menuhin became almost an annual fixture, while singers Joan Sutherland, Elisabeth Schwarzkopf, Maria Callas and Placido Domingo came to perform, along with dancers Margot Fonteyn and Rudolf Nureyev.

As the festivities have grown, Edinburgh has adapted accordingly, with an increasingly liberal attitude – and the city is open all night for at least four weeks of the year. Today several festivals take place concurrently during August (see box), while in winter the hugely popular **Hogmanay** festival culminates in New Year celebrations. Check out www.edinburghfestivalcity.com for details on the whole range of events.

Scottish National Gallery.

Tour 5

East Princes Street and Calton Hill

Starting between Edinburgh's Old and New Towns, this 2-mile (3km) walk takes in, in half a day, two of the city's best art galleries before climbing Calton Hill for stunning views

This tour explores the area developed as the city expanded beyond the Old Town, starting at The Mound, built across the chasm between old and new Edinburgh. By an Act of Parliament in 1816, authorisation to build here was granted through consultation with Princes Street residents, but with a guarantee that Princes Street Gardens should be preserved as open space (see box). It wasn't until 1830 that a proper road was constructed.

Beyond, the volcanic outcrop Calton Hill looms up at the eastern end of the New Town, offering grand views of the city and home to early 19th-century structures that reveal a great deal about its royal history.

Highlights

- Scottish National Gallery
- Scott Monument
- Calton Hill views and Monument
- Shopping on Broughton Street
- St Mary's Cathedral

Descending the hill's northern slope, fine Georgian architecture and Edinburgh's atmospheric St Mary's Roman Catholic Cathedral are both superb sights this side of the city.

ART ON THE MOUND

Between the towers of the former Bank of Scotland headquarters and Princes

Relaxing in the lovely Princes Street Gardens.

Street stands the splendid **Scottish National Gallery** ❶ (tel: 0131-624 6200; www.nationalgalleries.org; daily 10am–5pm, Thu until 7pm; free), which houses one of the best art collections in Europe. Impressionism and Post-Impressionism are represented by some well-known works by Monet, Cézanne, Degas and Van Gogh, and there are fine examples of many of the Old Masters, including Botticelli, Raphael, Rembrandt and Titian. The outstanding Scottish collection includes well-known works by Raeburn and Ramsey. On-going redevelopment has slowed owing to soaring costs, delaying the construction of new galleries, which are now due for completion in 2020.

In front of this magnificent building is the no-less-lavish **Royal Scottish Academy** ❷ (tel: 0131-225 6671; www.royalscottishacademy.org; Mon–Sat 10am–5pm, Sun noon–5pm; free), erected in 1826 and surmounted by a statue of Queen Victoria by

The Nor' Loch

Now the setting of Princes Street Gardens and Waverley train station, the loch was created in the 15th century as a defensive dammed moat, guarding against attack from the north. Through the years it degenerated into a disease-ridden dumping ground, and at least 150 people drowned in it, many of them alleged witches, ducked to test their guilt. The loch was contracted and drained by degrees from 1759, until the land was dry enough to plant with gardens in 1820.

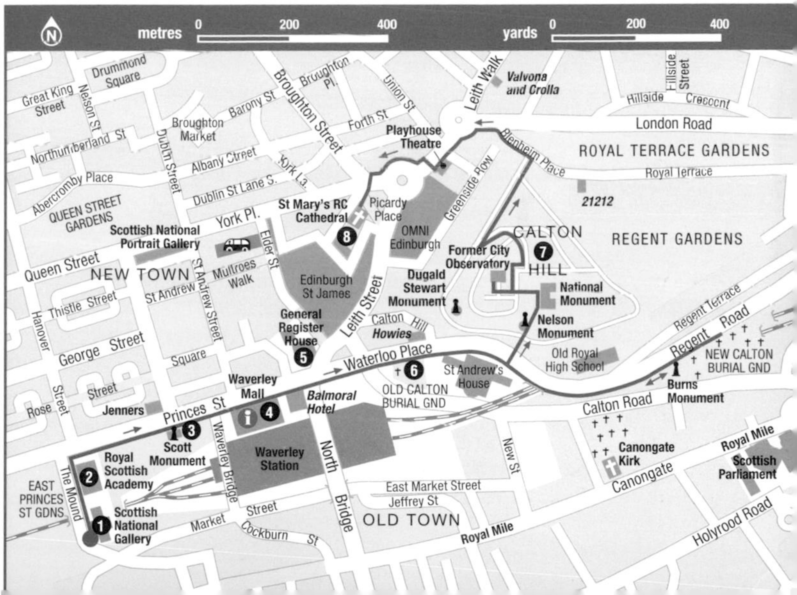

Shopping Haven

Princes Street remains Edinburgh's main shopping district, with a variety of predictable high-street shops alongside a few surprises, such as kilt makers Hector Russell at No. 95. **Jenners** at No. 48 first opened in 1838 and was the only independently owned Princes Street department store until it was bought by House of Fraser. At time of printing, Jenners' future was uncertain, following the House of Fraser chain going into administration. Other major department stores in the city include **Harvey Nichols** in St Andrew Square, while **John Lewis** is the anchor tenant in the redeveloped Edinburgh St James complex. **Waverley Mall** has a few high-street clothing outlets as well as **The Whisky Shop**, with its fine selection of Scotch whiskies.

Sir John Steell. The display rooms host temporary exhibitions of seminal painters and sculptors, as well as showcasing the best of the country's living traditional artists. Both galleries were designed by William Playfair, in addition to the adjacent flight of steps that leads to the top of the Mound. An entrance to the gallery complex, the **Weston Link**, leads directly inside from Princes Street Gardens.

ALONG PRINCES STREET

Turning eastwards along Princes Street (westwards is dealt with in Tour 6), itself named after the sons of King George III, you shortly notice the remarkable 200ft (61m) **Scott Monument** ❸ (tel: 0131-529 4068; www.edinburghmuseums.org.uk; daily Apr–Sep 10am–7pm (9pm in high season), Oct–Mar 10am–4pm, numbers are

The Balmoral Hotel.

limited, book online), begun eight years after the death of the novelist Sir Walter Scott, one of Edinburgh's most famous citizens, in 1832. Its daring mix of Gothic fantasy and pure romanticism was the work of George Meikle Kemp, the winner of an open architectural competition for the work. Sadly, Kemp was never to see his creation finished, having drowned in the Union Canal during its construction.

At the base of the monument is a statue of Sir Walter with Maida, his favourite staghound, but looking upwards the exterior incorporates more than 60 other statuettes of characters from his books. Climb the narrow, winding staircase of 287 steps for excellent views across the city.

Across Waverley Bridge, a statue of David Livingstone, the missionary and explorer, is set back in **East Princes Street Gardens**, while beyond is the figure of Adam Black, twice Lord Provost of Edinburgh and one-time member of parliament, and a statue of Professor John Wilson, who wrote popular articles under the pen-name of Christopher North.

Waverley

Until 1799 Princes Street was largely residential, but in 1846 local people asked William Playfair – whose hand is seen in almost every corner of the east end of Edinburgh – to mask a new and intruding modern railway line with a wall and embankment. Today this space is the site of the multi-level **Waverley Mall ❹**, a shopping centre with the tourist information office on the roof, while in the valley below is **Edinburgh Waverley**, the city's main train station.

Just beyond Waverley Mall, on the corner of Princes Street and North Bridge is the ultra-luxurious five-star **Balmoral Hotel**, built by Sir William Hamilton Beattie (who was also responsible for Jenners department store, see box) in over-elaborate Victorian style in 1902 and dominated by a large clock tower, revealing its former association with the Waverley railway. It's still the place to be seen enjoying afternoon tea at its stylish Palm Court café, and it also has two exclusive restaurants.

Directly opposite the Balmoral across North Bridge is the former General Post Office, the work of Robert Matheson in more distinguished classic style in 1861. Today called **Waverley Gate**, all that remains of the original building is the attractive outer shell: inside, modern design endows a large central atrium, extensive office space, basement parking and a roof garden.

Return of the Tram?

Almost 60 years after the closure of Edinburgh's city-wide double-decker tram system, electric trams have made a dramatic return to the city. The project, begun in 2008, was originally beset with problems, and the proposed budget more than doubled to around £900 million. The long-awaited tramline eventually opened in 2014, running from the airport to the city centre, and has fuelled a surge of investment in Princes Street; nearly five million passengers travelled on the trams during the first year of operations. Visit www.edinburghtrams.com for more details.

Register House

On the other side of Princes Street is **General Register House ❺** (tel: 0131-535 1314; www.nrscotland.gov.uk; Mon–Fri 9am–4.30pm; free), designed by Robert and James Adam in 1774, and the most important building on the street. The first major public building to go up in the New Town, it is one of the earliest purpose-built public records offices in the UK and incorporates 100 graceful vaulted rooms, divided by thick stone walls to protect Scotland's National Archives within. Rotating exhibitions on famous Scots and

Religious paintings at the Scottish National Gallery.

Wages of Waterloo

The early 19th-century eastward expansion of the New Town was a hugely ambitious and expensive project driven by a sense of national pride after the defeat of Napoleon. The scale of the achievement is visible on reaching the open section of Waterloo Place, where the drop to the Old Town is seen through triumphant arches – though the bridge took seven years to build and almost bankrupted Edinburgh. George IV made a grand entrance into the city from Calton Hill on his State visit in 1822, and Regent Terrace and Royal Terrace were named after him.

The Nelson Monument and the National Monument beyond it.

issues of national importance feature in the building's reception area, while genealogical research can be undertaken at the ScotlandsPeople Centre. The statue in front of the building is of the Duke of Wellington on horseback. Behind is the New Register House.

GAOL AND GRAVEYARD

Continuing eastwards onto **Waterloo Place** is the **Old Calton Burial Ground** ❻, in which lie many of the great names of the Scottish Enlightenment, including the philosopher David Hume. The obelisk, which was erected in 1844, commemorates exiled revolutionary Thomas Muir and several other political martyrs. George E Bissell's 1893 **Emancipation Monument**, depicting Abraham Lincoln with a freed slave kneeling at his feet, is in memory of the Scottish soldiers who died fighting in the American Civil War.

Next to the graveyard facing westwards is **St Andrew's House**, Thomas Tait's 1939 Art Deco structure that serves as the headquarters of the Scottish Government. It was built on the site of the Calton Jail, once Scotland's largest prison, though only the mock medieval tower, known as Governor's House, survives.

With Calton Hill looming above, beyond on Regent Road is the **Old**

New Town architecture.

Dugald Stewart Monument, Calton Hill.

Royal High School, a Greek Doric building designed by Thomas Hamilton in 1829, and though slated to be the location of the new Scottish Parliament, it was rejected on grounds of size in 1997. Nearby is the 1830 Greek-temple style **Burns Monument** – again designed by Thomas Hamilton – which also overlooks the **New Calton Burial Ground**, dating from 1821 and lying close to Holyrood Palace.

CALTON HILL

Calton Hill ❼, one of the city's best viewpoints, is topped with some grand buildings and is therefore very popular with visitors. The most attractive ascent up the hill is from Waterloo Place on its west side, though there are also paths from Blenheim Place or from next to the Playhouse Theatre via Greenside Row. From the top there are panoramic views of the Old and New Towns, Holyrood Palace, Arthur's Seat and the Firth of Forth, and because of this in summer many tourist coaches stop here. If you're driving, there is also limited parking at the top, with access from Royal Terrace. Most of the buildings, both on the hill's summit and below, date from just after the Napoleonic Wars, in which Scottish soldiers played a significant role.

Nelson Monument

On the south side of the hill is the **Nelson Monument** (tel: 0131-556 2716; www.edinburghmuseums.org.uk; daily, Sept 10am–7pm, Oct–Apr 10am–4pm, May 10am–7pm, Jun–Aug 10am–9pm), erected in 1807 to celebrate Admiral Nelson's naval victory at Trafalgar. It's worth climbing the spiral staircase to the lookout platform on a clear day for the great 360° views – try to be here at 1pm, when the one o'clock Time Ball is dropped to coincide with the gun fired from Edinburgh Castle.

With its sights trained on the length of Princes Street, a cannon squats defensively nearby, and to the west, the **Dugald Stewart Monument**, by William Playfair, commemorates a distinguished professor of philosophy at Edinburgh University. Crowning the summit is **Rock House**, the 19th-century former home of the pioneering photographer David Octavius Hill (1802–70).

National Monument

On the centre of the hill, the dozen grand pillars of the **National Monument** honour the soldiers killed in the Napoleonic Wars. It was intended that this should be a full-scale replica of the Parthenon in Athens, but only William Playfair's west side

The incomplete National Monument, known as 'Scotland's Shame'.

was completed before funds ran out, leading to its pseudonym 'Scotland's Shame'. Nonetheless, it's still an impressive, if somewhat foolhardy, feat of construction. Nearby, the Grecian theme is continued with the former **City Observatory**, also designed by Sir William Playfair in 1818, before the complex was moved to Blackford Hill, when new street lighting became too powerful to enable clear views of the stars here. The site has been redeveloped to house Collective, an arts centre and exhibition space.

PICARDY PLACE

Descend from Calton Hill on its northern side to meet **Blenheim Place**, a grand Georgian street above London Road and the Royal Terrace Gardens. The streets around the north and east slopes of the hill all exhibit majestic Georgian terraces, with William Playfair's Royal Terrace especially notable for its sets of seven, ten and a further seven giant Corinthian colonnades and balustrades, each set enclosing arched entrances and ground-floor windows.

Continuing to the main road, you shortly arrive at major city artery **Leith Walk**, a wide road running all the way from the centre to the port district of Leith with trees and wrought-iron work at its centre. The tone of the shops lining it varies tremendously – many are somewhat downmarket – though superb delicatessen and café **Valvona and Crolla** (see box) is worth a visit.

Heading westwards onto **Picardy Place**, the **Playhouse Theatre** (tel: 0844-871 3014), one of the city's largest venues for live entertainment, is on your left. On the other side of the place heading northwards, **Broughton Street** has gained a name for itself as both an alternative and gay district, with some excellent boutiques, art galleries, restaurants and food shops, as well as a number of cafés and bars, most equally straight-friendly as they are gay. Picardy Place was also the birthplace of Sherlock Holmes creator Sir Arthur Conan Doyle, hence the Conan Doyle pub opposite on the corner of York Place, with various Holmes-related displays.

Florist on Broughton Street.

The opulent interior of 21212.

St Mary's Cathedral

St Mary's Roman Catholic Cathedral ❽ (daily 8.30am–6pm; free), designed by James Gillespie Graham in 1813, was the first Catholic church to be built in Edinburgh after the Reformation, largely to accommodate Catholics displaced in the Highland clearances and Irish potato famine. A fire in 1878 left only the facade, but the early 20th-century interior is still atmospheric and worth a look. On the terracing in front of the cathedral, three statues include a giant foot and a hand by Sir Eduardo Paolozzi, born in 1924 in nearby Leith. These symbolise the strong connections between Edinburgh and the Italian families from Bargos and Monte Cassino, who arrived at the end of the 19th century.

Leith Street, connecting Picardy Place with Princes Street, is straddled by the **Edinburgh St James complex**, due for completion in 2020. On its eastern side is the Omni leisure complex with multi-screen cinema and health club. In front of it are two giant giraffe statues affectionately known as Martha and Gilbert.

Eating Out

21212
3 Royal Terrace; tel: 0131-523 1030; www.21212restaurant.co.uk; Tue–Sat lunch and dinner.
Paul Kitching's Michelin-starred restaurant is among the city's very best, balancing opulent period furnishings with modern touches and an informal ethic. French style and Scottish flavours combine in the innovative set menu, and though the choice of dishes is limited there's a new taste experience in every mouthful. £££

Howies
29 Waterloo Place; tel: 0131-556 5766; www.howies.uk.com; daily, lunch and dinner.
Very popular, locally owned group of unpretentious bistros serving modern Scottish dishes, including salmon, steak, chicken and fish of the day. Set in a fine Georgian building under Calton Hill. Good wine list or BYO. ££

Number One
Balmoral Hotel, 1 Princes Street; tel: 0131-557 6727; www.roccofortehotels.com; dinner only.
The Michelin-starred flagship restaurant of the Balmoral offers an exceptionally well-presented choice of Scottish and international flavours across the various menus that include a tasting option with specially chosen wines. The exclusive ambience is enhanced by contemporary art. Smart dress and booking essential. £££

Palm Court
Balmoral Hotel, 1 Princes Street; tel: 0131-556 2414; www.roccofortehotels.com; daily 9am–7pm, tea served noon–5pm.
The place to be seen for afternoon tea, with pastries, scones, smoked-salmon sandwiches and the like served in sumptuous surroundings under a glass dome and Venetian chandelier, accompanied by gentle harp music. £££

The Scottish Cafe & Restaurant
Scottish National Gallery, The Mound; tel: 0131-226 6524; www.contini.com; Mon–Sat 9am–5pm, Thu 9am–7pm, Sun 10am–5pm.
With great views over Princes Street Gardens and a lovely outdoor terrace, this is a good bet for morning coffee or lunch, although it can get very busy. ££

Valvona and Crolla
19 Elm Row (off Leith Walk); tel: 0131-556 6066; www.valvonacrolla.co.uk; Mon–Thu 8.30am–5.30pm, Fri–Sat 8am–8.30pm, Sun 10.30am–4.30pm.
A superb option for coffee, lunch or a glass of wine at Edinburgh's oldest and most famous delicatessen. Delicious Italian-Scottish food is freshly prepared to family recipes. £

Princes Street Gardens.

Tour 6

West Princes Street and New Town

This tour begins halfway along Princes Street and explores the architecture of the Georgian New Town. To walk the tour suggested is a full day, covering about 4–5 miles (8km)

The New Town of Edinburgh is an elegant commercial and residential area that has been awarded World Heritage Site status. It is built on a grid system of wide avenues of 18th- and 19th-century buildings running in parallel. Any walk here should take in the area north of Queen Street – there are no visitor attractions as such, but the appeal is to fans of superb residential architecture.

From the parallel Princes, George and Queen streets, the New Town drops downhill towards Stockbridge, Comely Bank and Inverleith, encompassing the pattern of squares and crescents devised in James Craig's award-winning 18th-century plan.

Highlights

- Floral Clock
- Georgian House
- St Mary's Episcopal Cathedral
- New Town architecture
- Scottish National Portrait Gallery

PRINCES STREET GARDENS

From the foot of the Mound opposite the National Gallery, this walk begins at the western section of **Princes Street Gardens**, where the world's oldest **Floral Clock** ❶ keeps time with electric-driven hands and laid out annually with over 20,000 plants. The gardens were planted in the valley below the Castle Rock after (then residential) Princes Street won the battle to keep its view of the Old Town skyline. Developers gave up their plans to build in the space left after the Nor' Loch was drained, and though exceptions were later made for Waverley Station, the railway line, and the Scott Monument in the East Gardens, the view is still unspoiled. Initially intended for the exclusive use of residents, the gardens are today open to all.

A number of statues line the gardens, including poet Allan Ramsay (by Sir John Steell), Sir Frank Mears' memorial to the Royal Scots, who according to legend served with Pontius Pilate's bodyguard in Scotland, and further along, Birnie Rhind's equestrian statue paying tribute to the Royal Scots Greys. The most recent memorial is by Ian Hamilton Finlay, the 'concrete poet', which honours Robert Louis Stevenson. Beyond, the **Ross Open-Air Theatre** (tel: 0131-228 8616) is a popular summer venue, well used for concerts and dancing during the Edinburgh Festival.

Strolling through Princes Street Gardens.

Garden Churches

At the West End of Princes Street Gardens on the corner with Lothian Road is **St John's Episcopal Church** ❷ (Mon–Sat 9am–5.30pm, Sun 8am–7pm; free), designed by William Burn in 1818 and partly modelled on St George's Chapel in Windsor. Its interior celebrates the Gothic revival in Scotland, with superb stained-glass windows.

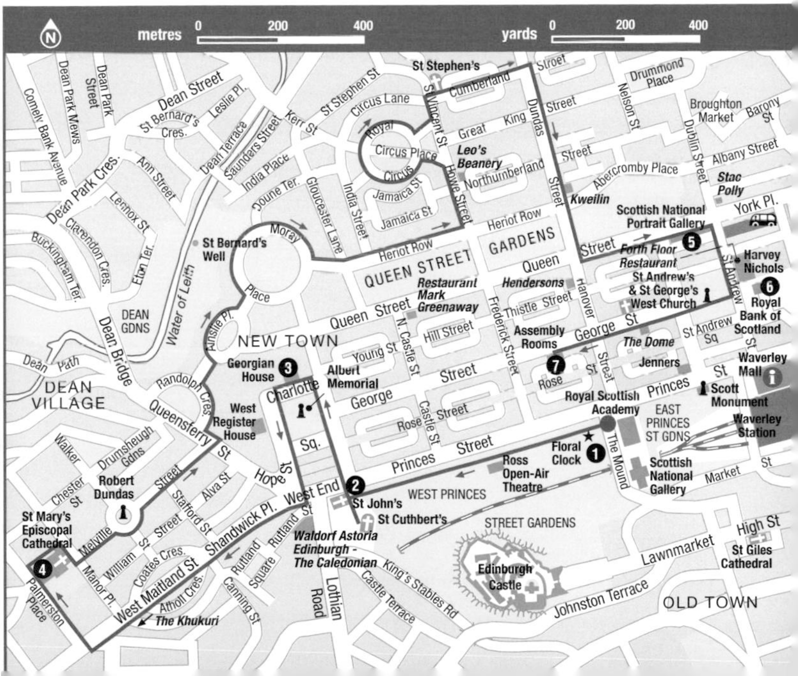

The floral clock in Princes Street Gardens.

Tucked away behind St John's is **St Cuthbert's Kirk** (Apr–Sept Mon–Fri 10am–3.30pm, Sat 10am–1pm, Oct–Mar Tue–Thu 10am–3pm; free), built in 1894 on the site of a series of older churches and monastery going back as far as the 8th century. Inside, murals by John Duncan and a fresco of St Cuthbert on Lindisfarne are notable, though it's the eerie kirkyard that probably holds most interest. By the mid-18th century grave-robbing had become such a common occurrence here that the extra high walls were built and night watchmen were introduced – nonetheless, the graves of Alexander Nasmyth, the painter George Meikle Kemp (ill-fated designer of the Scott Monument) and Thomas de Quincey, author of *Confessions of an Opium Eater*, are all allegedly still here.

St Cuthbert's Kirk.

CHARLOTTE SQUARE

Walk one block northwards to stunning **Charlotte Square**, considered the finest square in the city, with a central garden featuring the equestrian **Albert Memorial** statue by Sir John Steell. The gardens are only available to owners of the surrounding properties, but during the last three weeks in August they play host to the Edinburgh International Book Festival, when an estimated 220,000 visitors fill the tented gardens to hear from a host of well-known and up-and-coming authors from around the world.

Designed by Robert Adam in 1791, the square is named after Queen Charlotte, the wife of George III and the mother of his 15 children. The north side is viewed as Adam's greatest neoclassical urban masterpiece, and its exclusive status is assured today in the form of **Bute House**, the official residence of the First Minister of the Scottish Government at No. 6.

On the west side a branch of the National Records of Scotland is set in domed **West Register House**, originally St George's Church. In 2013 the south side was redeveloped, creating new office space behind a restored series of townhouses.

Georgian House at No. 7.

Georgian House

The three floors of No. 7, **Georgian House** ❸ (tel: 0844-493 2118; www.nts.org.uk/visit/places/Georgian-House; daily Apr–Oct 10am–5pm, Nov–mid-Dec, Mar 11am–4pm; closed Mon–Wed Dec) were formerly owned by the family of the Marquess of Bute and have been refurbished by the National Trust in the style of the late 18th-century. There is a fascinating array of china, silver, pictures, furniture, gadgets and utensils ranging from the decorative to the purely functional, and adjacent to an imaginative museum shop is an audio-visual room describing the lives of the wealthy inhabitants of Edinburgh's New Town.

THE WEST END

Back at the West End of Princes Street, the commanding **Waldorf Astoria Edinburgh – The Caledonian hotel** stands on the south side, built as a railway hotel rivalling the Balmoral when there was a station at either end of Princes Street. As you continue west for 0.25 miles (0.4km) along **Shandwick Place**, striking Georgian **Atholl Crescent** and **Coates Crescent** are as far west as the original planned New Town extended, with a statue of Britain's prime minister William Gladstone (1809–98) out in front.

Exile of the Rich

Before the New Town was built from the 1760s onwards, the rising population of Edinburgh was confined within the cramped space around the Royal Mile, where tenements rose to 10 or 11 storeys and were shared by the rich and the poor. After the New Town was established, the city's social stratification was for the first time reflected in its geographical division, as those who could afford to hauled their possessions across the Mound to this spacious northern suburb.

Haymarket railway station lies beyond, at the end of West Maitland Street.

St Mary's Episcopal Cathedral

Turn right onto Palmerston Place (named after the Third Viscount Palmerston, British Prime Minister in the 19th century) to arrive at stunning **St Mary's Episcopal Cathedral** ❹ (daily 7.15am–6pm, until 9pm in summer; free), the largest church built in Scotland since the Reformation, with distinctive spires on the Edinburgh skyline. Designed by Sir George Gilbert Scott in 1879, it was funded by a legacy from Barbara and Mary Walker, two spinster ladies and the heiresses of Sir Pat-

Ornate window on a house in Charlotte Square.

Sprawling New Town in the mist.

rick Walker (1777–1837), a wealthy advocate and landowner. Walk around the church on its northern side to admire the quaint 18th-century Walkers' family cottages, now housing the renowned **St Mary's Music School**.

At the northeastern end of the cathedral **Melville Street** and **Melville Crescent**, both designed by Robert Brown in 1814, proudly display a statue of Robert Dundas, by John Steell, at their centre.

The imposing facade of the Waldorf Astoria Edinburgh – The Caledonian.

THE SECOND NEW TOWN

The substantial sweeping architectural masterpieces of the second New Town, largely defined as the area north of **Queen Street**, were designed for Edinburgh's professional classes, with servants' quarters sometimes located at the end of streets and stable accommodation behind. Except for a few hotel developments and some offices, nearly all the town houses are now divided into flats, with the big, railed gardens of Moray Place, Royal Circus and Queen Street unfortunately open to key-holding residents only. Most of the streets exhibit similar styles, with the suggested route below covering some of the most important architecture.

From **Queensferry Street** – which initiates the first stage of the main road towards the Firth of Forth crossing – take an immediate right into impressive **Randolph Crescent**, named after Sir Thomas Randolph (d. 1332), Robert the Bruce's nephew. Built in the 1820s, the crescent showcases ornate arched doorways with Roman Doric pilasters, an architectural effort that continues down into **Ainslie Place**, named after the 10th

Architectural Showpiece

One of the greatest achievements of the Scottish Enlightenment was the creation of Edinburgh's New Town, complementing the narrow wynds (alleys) of the medieval city. The architectural masterpiece that followed was the result of a competition held in 1767 and won by 22-year-old James Craig. Craig's design favoured a grid system, creating the largest and finest showpiece of Georgian architecture next to Bath.

Influenced by the Palladian style, William Adam, and his sons Robert and James, among others, began designing the classical squares and crescents of the **first New Town**, which evolved up to 1791, while the **second New Town** was laid out to the north of the first, on the steep slope towards the Water of Leith, by Robert Reid. The latter concentrated on Great King Street, leading to Royal Circus, designed by William Playfair, and westwards, the Moray Estate with its 12-sided Moray Place, which was completed on an interlinking system by James Gillespie Graham.

Earl of Moray's second wife, Margaret Ainslie of Pilton.

Moray Place and Heriot Row

Beyond, **Moray Place** is one of Edinburgh's most prestigious residential addresses, with a 12-sided design by James Gillespie Graham, built on land once owned by Mary, Queen of Scots' illegitimate brother, the Earl of Moray.

Heading eastwards, **Heriot Row** continues the ultra-grand New Town ambience. Built by Robert Reid in 1802 with additions by David Bryce in 1864, the street is named after George Heriot, who bankrolled James VI on his journey to London. In 1857, No. 17 (marked by brass plates) became the home of Thomas Stevenson, father of the writer Robert Louis Stevenson, whose childhood memories here inspired *Treasure Island* (1881) and his poem, *The Lamplighter*. In the late 19th century the novelist commented on the decay of parts of the New Town, hard to believe as today's World Heritage Site: *'It is as much a matter of course to decry the New Town as to exalt the Old; and the most celebrated authorities have picked out this quarter as the very emblem of what is condemned in architecture'*.

Royal Circus to Dundas Street

Below Heriot Row, **Howe Street** (named after the celebrated admiral of the Seven Years' War, Richard, First Earl Howe) leads down towards the two-winged **Royal Circus**, added by William Playfair in 1822, and around the corner at the foot of Howe Street, sprawling **St Stephen's Church** was built by the same architect in 1827. The impressiveness of wide avenues

Georgian building in the New Town.

Cumberland Street, **Fettes Row**, **Northumberland Street** and **Great King Street** (designed by Robert Reid in 1802) is not dampened by the terraces' palpable need of cleaning; all lead eastwards to **Drummond Place**.

All the streets heading north from Queen Street reflect the period of their creation, with **Dundas Street** (now superb for browsing its antiques shops and private art galleries), begun in 1807, named after Henry Dundas, First Viscount Melville (1742–1811), whose statue stands in St Andrew Square. **Abercromby Place**, designed by Robert Reid in 1805, overlooks **Queen Street Gardens** and is named after Sir Ralph Abercromby (1734–1801), hero of the Seven Years' War (1756–63).

CENTRAL STREETS AND SQUARES

As seemed appropriate for a major Georgian city, north sloping streets from Princes Street upwards were named after the reigning Hanoverian monarchy: **Frederick Street**, after George III's father, and **Hanover Street**, commemorating the six Hanoverian monarchs prior to the reign of Queen Victoria. **North** and **South St David Street** honour the patron saint of Wales, and St Andrew Square is named after the patron saint of Scotland, crucified on a diagonal cross that was to inspire the white cross on a blue background of the Scottish flag.

Scottish National Portrait Gallery

National Portrait Gallery entrance.

National Portrait Gallery

Queen Street, which runs parallel to Abercromby Place and George Street, was named after George III's wife, Queen Charlotte. At the east end is the **Scottish National Portrait Gallery** ❺ (tel: 0131-624 6200; www.nationalgalleries.org; daily 10am–5pm). The Gothic splendour of the external red sandstone houses within fine portraits of celebrated Scots including Robert Burns by Alexander Nasmyth, Robert Louis Stevenson by Count Nerlie, Mary, Queen of Scots by Peter Oudry, and more contemporary portraits such as the comedian Billy Connolly and author Ian Rankin.

Designed by Robert Rowand Anderson in 1890, the building was a gift to the Scottish nation from JR Finlay, who owned *The Scotsman* newspaper. Look out for the magnificent restored

Harvey Nichols Foodmarket, St Andrew Square.

murals on the front hall ceiling, by Phoebe Traquair.

St Andrew Square

Much altered by modern buildings, **St Andrew Square** still retains a few original facades such as the head office of the **Royal Bank of Scotland** ❻ on its east side, where much of the recent revamp of the square has taken place. Originally the home of Sir Laurence Dundas, a wealthy member of parliament who reputedly gambled away his home in a game of poker, it was designed by William Chambers and purchased by the bank in 1825, who promptly added a magnificent domed hall that features on their bank notes. The equestrian statue to the front depicts the Fourth Earl of Hopetoun, a hero of the Napoleonic Wars and a governor of the bank.

The square's centre is dominated by the 121ft (37m) **Melville Monument**, a Doric column surmounted by a statue by Robert Forrest of Henry Dundas, First Viscount Melville, who, as a key figure in Pitt the Younger's government, influenced Scottish politics to the extent that

New Town Retail Therapy

The New Town shopping district extends through George and Princes streets and from Castle Street to the revamped St Andrew Square. The latter square boasts designer department store **Harvey Nichols** and Multrees Walk shopping enclave. Parallel to Princes Street and George streets, Thistle Street abounds with independent **boutiques** and **antiques shops**, while further north on Dundas and Howe streets are the city's best smaller **art galleries** and antiques shops.

For excellent Scottish jewellery try Sheila Fleet at 18 St Stephen Street, Hamilton & Inches at 87 George Street or Rock Candy at 111 Rose Street (contemporary styles). For the persistent trawler, Unicorn Antiques at 65 Dundas Street is a delightful antiques and bric-à-brac shop.

For **tartan and kilts** the top names here are Stewart Christie at 63 Queen Street, and Hugh Macpherson at 17 West Maitland Street (accessed from 5a Grosvenor Street around the corner). Further afield, the kilt makers to the Royal Family are Kinloch Anderson, based at 4 Dock Street by Commercial Street in Leith.

The Royal Bank of Scotland in St Andrew Square.

The domed Royal Society of Edinburgh building on George Street.

he became known as 'The Uncrowned King of Scotland'.

George Street

Leading westwards from St Andrew Square, **George Street** (named after George III) features traditional shops interspersed with upmarket fashion stores and smart bars and restaurants. **St Andrew's and St George's West Church** (Mon–Fri 10am–3pm, Sat 11am–2pm, Sun 9am–3pm; free) was constructed in 1781–83, again to a competition-winning design. A sign on the facade explains that this was the scene of the 1843 General Assembly of the Church of Scotland, from which 470 evangelical ministers walked out to set up the Free Church, irrevocably changing the face of religion in Scotland. Opposite, a grander classical edifice, **The Dome**, was formerly a bank but is now a fashionable bar with an extravagant 19th-century interior.

Proud to be Scottish.

Statues at George Street's intersections honour a number of famous historical figures: Dr Thomas Chalmers, first principal of Free Church College, at Castle Street; William Pitt, the British prime minister, at Frederick Street, and George IV at Hanover Street. On the north side, between Hanover and Frederick streets, are the **Assembly Rooms** ❼, originating from 1818 but with a **Music Hall** added later. With their magnificent crystal chandeliers, the Assembly Rooms have been the venue for many a great social occasion and are now used as a Festival Fringe and occasional venue for events.

Eating Out

The Dome
14 George Street; tel: 0131-624 8624; www.thedomeedinburgh.com; Grill Room daily noon–late; Club Room Mon–Thu 10am–4pm and Fri–Sat from 10am; Georgian Tea Room (daily 10am–5pm).
This palatial former bank has many guises: a very popular and grand bar with a great cocktail list; a smarter 'Grill Room' for Scottish-orientated lunch and dinner; the Club Room for a less formal, less expensive meal and the Georgian Tea Room. £–£££

Forth Floor Restaurant
Harvey Nichols, St Andrew Square; tel: 0131 524 8350; Tue–Sat noon–2.30pm, 5.30–10pm.
This elegant space is on the fourth floor, but the name is a pun on its great views of the Firth. It's also a great choice for afternoon tea or for a cheaper daily lunch option at the Brasserie. £££

Hendersons
94 Hanover Street; tel: 0131-225 2131; www.hendersonsofedinburgh.co.uk; Mon–Thu 8.30am–8.45pm, Fri–Sat until 9.15pm, Sun 10.30am–4pm.
Established in 1962 (and staking a claim to be the UK's longest-running vegetarian restaurant), this vegetarian diner has a changing menu of fresh ingredients – try the jackfruit and mushroom burger or the vegetarian haggis. Plus there's live jazz most evenings. £

The Khukuri
8 West Maitland Street; tel: 0131-228 2085; www.thekhukuri.com; daily noon–11pm.
Khukuri has been serving flavoursome, authentic Nepalese cuisine since 1997. The staff will help you with choices, and there is a great selection for vegetarians. Takeaway is available, too.
£

Kweilin
19–21 Dundas Street; tel: 0131-557 1875; www.kweilin.net; Tue–Sat lunch and dinner.
For many the best Chinese in town, serving authentic Cantonese that showcases Scotland's glorious variety of fresh seafood. Set menus for two are available. ££

Leo's Beanery
23a Howe Street, tel: 0131-556 8403; www.leosbeanery.co.uk; Mon–Fri 8am–5pm, Sat 9am–5pm, Sun 10am–5pm.
A family-run café, where the aroma of freshly baked breads and cakes fills the air and quality produce is upmost. Dark wood furnishings and wholesome meals add to the comfort factor. £

Restaurant Mark Greenaway
69 North Castle Street; tel: 0131-226 1155; www.markgreenaway.com; Tue–Sat lunch and dinner.
Greenaway applies his signature modern style to classic French food, made with locally sourced, seasonal Scottish produce. The regularly changing menu consists of four courses, with a choice of two dishes for each course. £££

Stac Polly
29–33 Dublin Street; tel: 0131-556 2231; www.stacpolly.com; daily from 6pm.
This tastefully themed, Bute tweed-upholstered restaurant offers modern and traditional cuisine such as a twice-baked goats' cheese soufflé starter and crispy fillet of sea bream with chive rösti main.
£££

The splendid Tropical Palms glasshouse at the Royal Botanic Garden.

Tour 7

Water of Leith to Stockbridge and Dean

Probably the most interesting walk within the city limits, this 4 mile (6.5km) walk takes in pretty riverbanks, hidden villages and two superb galleries of modern art

This tour begins at Canonmills, close to the East Gate of the Royal Botanic Garden – Lothian bus services 23 and 27 from Hanover Street stop on Inverleith Row. Allow 2–3 hours plus time in the galleries. Most of the route is a pleasant stroll along the path beside the most interesting section of the **Water of Leith**, passing through Stockbridge, upriver to Dean Village, and onwards to the art galleries.

Highlights

- Royal Botanic Garden
- Water of Leith Walkway
- Stockbridge
- Dean Village
- Scottish National Gallery of Modern Art

CANONMILLS TO ST BERNARD'S WELL

The route begins at the start of Inverleith Row at **Canonmills**, where the Canons of Holyrood Abbey, granted lands by David I in the 12th century established a water mill on the Water of Leith. Writer Robert Louis Stevenson was born close to here in 1850 and spent much of his childhood in the Inverleith area, where he used to go fishing on the river. The wonderful **Royal Botanic Garden** ❶

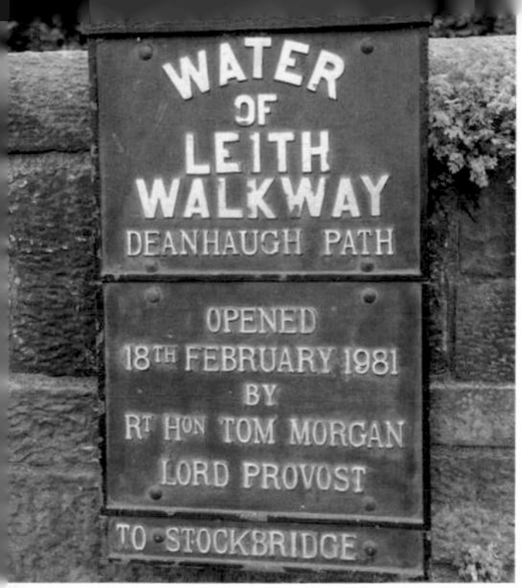

A sign on the Water of Leith Walkway.

The Water of Leith

At Slateford, in the southwestern suburbs, the Water of Leith Conservation Trust has opened a Visitor Centre by the river (24 Lanark Road; tel: 0131-455 7367; www.waterofleith.org.uk; daily 10am–4pm; free). Exhibits trace the history of the Water of Leith's past industrial role and illustrate its natural history and the Trust's conservation work.

(tel: 0131-248 2909; www.rbge.org.uk; daily Mar–Sept 10am–6pm, Nov–Jan until 4pm, Feb and Oct until 5pm; free, charge for glasshouses) is nearby, accessed from its East Gate on Inverleith Row, and can easily keep you occupied for a couple of hours with its Rock and Chinese gardens, Arboretum and Glasshouse.

Turn westwards onto the **Water of Leith Walkway**. Edinburgh's major natural waterway is an attractive

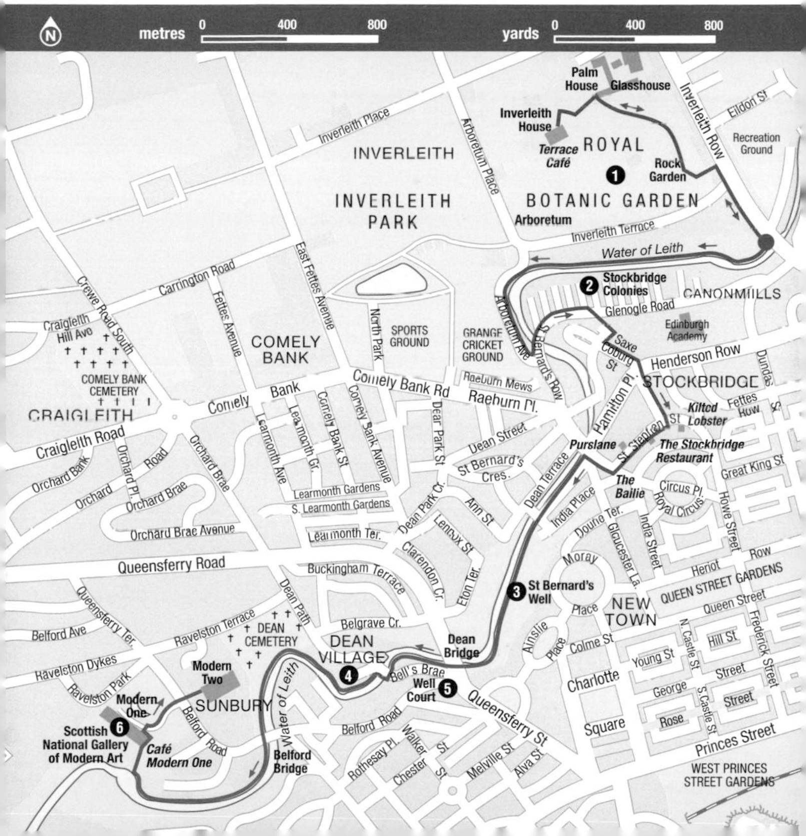

Stunning Dean Village is nestled in a leafy gorge below Dean Bridge.

ribbon of silver and green that begins in the Pentland Hills to the southwest and snakes through the city to the Firth of Forth at Leith. In recent years the riverside walkway has been lovingly restored by the Water of Leith Conservation Trust, and fish and flora have returned (see box).

You then emerge onto **Arboretum Avenue**, which was formerly the entrance to Inverleith House, itself built for the Rocheid family and which now stands at the centre of the Botanic Gardens. Just to the west is **Inverleith Park**, a popular area for football, rugby, tennis and cricket.

Stockbridge

Continue following the river for a few minutes and cross over it at Falshaw Bridge, erected in 1877, to reach the **Stockbridge Colonies** ❷, an 1860s housing development in an idyllic setting beside the river on Glenogle Road. These 11 rows of terraced houses were designed for artisans serving the New Town, and the gable ends of each block feature stone carvings of tools and implements belonging to the different trades of its residents.

Stockbridge itself is named after the footbridge spanning the river originally used by livestock; nowadays, it is a bustling shopping and residential centre to the northwest of the New Town. Half way along its neat rows of cottages, turn right onto the cobbled walkway leading to narrow Saxe Coburg Street, which finds its way through to Henderson Row. Just east along the street is the pristine, neoclassical **Edinburgh Academy** erected in 1824 by private subscription to a design by William Burn, to provide education for the sons of the New Town (daughters were regarded as being less worthy of serious education). A block further south adjoining North West Circus Place, is **St Stephen Street**, and much of the surrounding district heading north up to Raeburn Place is filled with interesting craft, curio and antiques shops, and cafés and bars.

A painting by Joan Miró in the Scottish National Gallery of Modern Art.

St Bernard's Well

Turn right onto Deanhaugh Street, where another, more recent, stone bridge crosses the river. Steps lead back down to the prettiest section of the Water of Leith (also accessed at the end of India Place), where private Dean Gardens span its western bank, and **St Bernard's Well** ❸, on its east – a small, circular 'Roman temple' with a statue of Hygeia, the Greek goddess of health. Folklore has it that the spring was discovered by three schoolboys fishing in the river in 1760, and thereafter it became popular for the supposed healing powers of its mineral water. A plaque acknowledges the purchase and restoration of the well by the publisher William Nelson, who bequeathed it to the city in 1888.

DEAN VILLAGE

Beyond the well the towering, four-arched **Dean Bridge**, built in 1832, looms overhead. Rising 106ft (32m) above the river, the bridge had a morbid reputation as a popular suicide spot until the parapets were raised in 1912. Further on **Dean Village** ❹ is a gem of cobbled streets and converted warehouses nestled away in a sunken hollow out of sight from the high town above. *Dean* means 'deep valley', and the Water of Leith Walkway skirts the whole base of the steep gorge, on its way passing the **Damhead Weir**, a rush of bubbling water that used to power the mills that ranged along this stretch of river.

Prior to the building of the Dean Bridge, people going towards Queensferry to the north of the city would have had to descend the street Bell's Brae and cross the old bridge in the village to climb up the steep far side of the gorge. An interesting diversion – if you can handle the climb – is to walk up Bell's Brae to **Well Court** ❺, a surprising square of red Teutonic-style

Best of Britain

Stockbridge grew largely under the influence of Henry Raeburn, the great Scottish portrait painter. As part of a commercial housing development, from 1813 onwards, and as a birthday present for his wife, he built the elegant and leafy Ann Street (which, unusually, features front gardens), once described by the English poet Sir John Betjeman as 'the most attractive street in Britain'.

residential buildings with a clock tower. The square was a Victorian experiment in community dwelling by the philanthropist JR Findlay, proprietor of *The Scotsman* newspaper.

The site of the village was first granted to the canons of Holyrood in 1143, and at one time the Baker's Guild ran 11 water mills here, manufacturing all the meal for the region. The industry went into rapid decline when larger, modern mills opened in Leith during the 19th century, and similarly, the Dean Tannery that once processed sheepskins was demolished in 1973. These days, the picturesque, secluded hideaway has assured substantial residential building – with hefty prices to match.

Dean Cemetery

Crossing Bell's Brae, Hawthornbank Lane leads to a footbridge over the

St Bernard's Well.

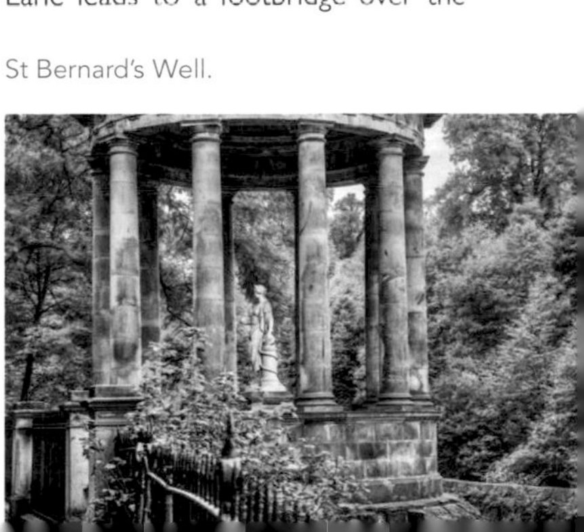

The neoclassical building of the Scottish National Gallery of Modern Art.

ancient ford, where the walkway continues a short way around the corner on the northern side of the river. Access to the **Dean Cemetery** (daily 9am–5pm, until dusk in winter), laid out in the grounds of demolished Dean House, is from Dean Path, another uphill diversion. Among the prominent Edinburgh citizens interred here are such seminal names as Lord Cockburn, WH Playfair, the painter Sam Bough, the photographer David Octavius Hill and Dr Elsie Inglis, who founded the Scottish Women's Suffragette Movement. In a charming location above the river, the cemetery is noted for its fine collection of sculptures and architectural monuments.

Eduardo Paolozzi's studio at the Scottish National Gallery of Modern Art.

SCOTTISH NATIONAL GALLERY OF MODERN ART

A steep flight of steps leads back down to the riverbank from Dean Path, while a few hundred yards farther along the walkway, the 1887 **Belford Bridge** marks the start of its Dean Bank section. The Walkway continues westwards from here 3 miles (5km) to the Coltbridge Viaduct, which now carries a cycleway on along the former Balerno railway line. Less than half a mile (0.5km) from the bridge, in a lush, deep section of the glen, however, is the **Scottish National Gallery of Modern Art** ❻ (tel: 0131-624 6200; www.nationalgalleries.org; daily 10am–5pm; free), accessed by marked steps from the Water of Leith.

Scotland's national collection of 20th-century paintings, sculptures and graphics was founded in 1959 and located at Inverleith House in the Royal Botanic Garden until 1984. The inspiring collection then moved here and is now housed in two neoclassical buildings known as Modern One and Modern Two.

Modern One's building, which was designed in 1825 as John Watson's Hospital and School, features works by major British, European and American 20th-century and 21st-century artists – highlights include paintings

Eating Out

The Bailie

2–4 St Stephen Street, Stockbridge; tel: 0131-225 4673; www.thebailiebar.co.uk; food served Mon–Sat 11am–10pm, Sun 12.30–10pm.

This traditional and cosy cellar pub has great ales, fine malt whiskies and a regular clientele, while the pub food (roast dinners, sandwiches, salads and steaks) is of a good standard. ££

Café Modern One

Scottish National Gallery of Modern Art, 75 Belford Road; tel: 0131-332 8600; daily 10am–4.30pm.

An excellent stop for coffee, self-service lunch or afternoon tea, especially if the weather allows you to sit outside and admire the landscaped gardens. Veggie options. £

Kilted Lobster

112 St Stephen Street, Stockbridge; tel: 0131-220 6677; www.kiltedlobster.com; Mon, Wed–Fri dinner, Sat lunch and dinner, Sun noon–8pm.

Since opening its doors in 2015, this primarily seafood restaurant with nautical motifs has built a fine reputation for its delicious no-frills cooking. There's everything from chowders to oysters and langoustines to sea bream, but meat eaters catered for too. ££

Purslane

33a St Stephen Street; tel: 0131-226 3500; www.purslanerestaurant.co.uk; Tue–Sun lunch and dinner.

Casual fine dining is how this restaurant markets itself. Superbly prepared locally produced food – around 80 percent is sourced locally – is imaginatively presented. This is one of Edinburgh's best restaurants. £££

The Stockbridge Restaurant

54 St Stephen Street, Stockbridge; tel: 0131-226 6766; www.thestockbridgerestaurant.co.uk; Tue–Sun dinner only, also Sat, Sun lunch.

Raising the level of Stockbridge cuisine in one easy stroke, this fine basement restaurant has a seasonal menu with delicious dishes such as rabbit loin wrapped in serrano ham, and halibut with crab and scallop mousse. £££

Terrace Café

Royal Botanic Gardens, Inverleith Row; tel: 0131-552 0606; daily 10am–4.15pm, until 5.15pm in summer.

At the centre of the tranquil gardens the Terrace tends to be a little hectic on warmer days, when visitor numbers are high, but it's a good bet for afternoon tea or a lunch of British favourites. Also licensed for alcohol. £

by Matisse and Picasso. Work from David Hockney and Andy Warhol sit alongside more recent work by Damien Hirst and Tracey Emin. Scottish art is also strongly represented.

The pond-lined parklands are dotted with sculptures by important artists including Henry Moore, Barbara Hepworth, Jacob Epstein and Nathan Coley.

Providing additional space for the collection, on the far side of Belford Road, Modern Two (the former Dean Gallery) occupies a striking Baroque-style building with a two-storey attic on top of the portico, which features the clock of the old Netherbow. Built by Thomas Hamilton in 1833 as an Orphan Hospital, today it hosts a changing programme of exhibitions and displays drawn from the permanent collection. Don't miss the recreation of Eduardo Paolozzi's studio, as well as his huge sculpture, *Vulcan*, which dominates the café.

Botanic Oasis

Relax at Edinburgh's Royal Botanic Garden, an astonishing collection of indigenous and global plants and ecosystems, with a lot more to see besides

Amidst the frenetic festival atmosphere of Edinburgh in August, there is no better place to relax than the **Royal Botanic Garden** (tel: 0131-248 2909; www.rbge.org.uk; daily Mar–Sept 10am–6pm, Nov–Jan until 4pm, Feb and Oct until 5pm; free, but glasshouses have an entrance charge and close at 5pm in summer and at 3pm in winter), an easy stroll north of the New Town.

THE GARDEN LAYOUT

Set across 70 acres (28 hectares) of superb landscaping, including exotic, beautiful and bizarre plants, this world-famous garden evolved from the Physic Gardens established near Holyrood Abbey in 1670, and has been on its present site since 1820. There is a constant cycle of redeveloping, landscaping and seasonal replanting, which means there are always special attractions, whatever time of year you visit.

A network of footpaths lead you on a journey of exploration through magnificent colours and rock pools, with the **Chinese garden** a particular highlight, featuring a large collection mainly from southwest China. There are also indigenous areas, such as a Highland heath with traditional peat walls, and nearby

Looking out from the Chinese Hillside.

woodland that take you into a replica northern Scotland. Some of the finest rhododendrons in the UK – sourced from as far afield as Borneo – are to be found in the separate Woodland Gardens, and throughout, medicinal plants are labelled, no doubt a relic from the Gardens' founder, Sir Robert Sibbald, physician to Charles II and first Professor of Medicine at Edinburgh University.

The **Glasshouses** are the main attraction for many, however. In fact, 10 separate Victorian constructions, the tropical and temperate palm houses are the largest of their kind worldwide and particularly spectacular – though the steamy orchid house with its giant water lilies is also impressive.

Leading up towards the gardens from Stockbridge, Arboretum Avenue was formerly the entrance to **Inverleith House**, a Georgian mansion house standing at the centre of the gardens, which now operates as an art gallery featuring temporary exhibitions and events. One of the best panoramic views of the city's skyline can be enjoyed from its back lawn, while all around is the area traditionally known as **The Arboretum**, with trees grouped by their botanical family.

EATING AND SHOPPING

The **Terrace Café**, next to Inverleith House, serves good teas and light meals, while the **Gateway Restaurant**, located at the **John Hope Gateway biodiversity and information centre** at the gardens' West Gate entrance, has a more upmarket menu. Also here is an interactive exhibition on the scientific work of the gardens and the **Botanics Shop**, which stocks gifts, gardening equipment, seeds and bulbs, plus an outdoor plant sales area.

PRACTICAL INFORMATION

Allow half a day for your visit – this is a great spot for picnics. Garden Guides offer visitors hour-long tours (Apr–Oct 11am and 2pm) of plant collections and seasonal highlights, with information on the gardens' history and global linkages. To get here, hop on Lothian bus services 8, 23 or 27 from Hanover Street and stop at the East Gate on Inverleith Row, though also consider hiring bikes to arrive here, as cycle racks are provided at the north and east gates.

The Shore at sunset.

Tour 8

Leith

Lying on the Firth of Forth, Leith is Edinburgh's historical port and has had a resurgence in recent decades. Plan for half a day in Leith, then lunch in one of the area's great restaurants

First recorded in 1143, Leith served as Scotland's foremost port from the 14th to the mid-19th centuries, trading with much of northern Europe and twice suffering destructive English attacks in the 16th century. In 1548, Catholic Mary of Guise, Governor of Scotland during her daughter Mary, Queen of Scots' infancy, made it her seat of government, and, when threatened by the anti-Catholic sentiments that led to the Reformation, she raised fortifications to defend the town. After her death two years later, the triumphant Protestants pulled them down, but Leith remained discrete from Edinburgh for most of its later history.

Despite the mid-17th century plague that killed almost two-thirds of Leith's population, the port remained at the forefront of shipping until the early 19th century, when it fell into a long decline. Incorporation with Edinburgh was forced on Leith in 1920, but the town retained a fierce individuality, with many old Leithers even today not considering themselves citizens of the wider city. Despite this feeling for tradition, a massive programme of renovation and urban redevelopment has taken place since the early 1980s, and Leith, once seen as a sleazy port

Highlights

- Leith Links, birthplace of golf
- Bernard Street and The Shore
- Ocean Terminal and the Royal Yacht Britannia

Royal Sport

Leith Links lays claim to an even longer history as a golf course than the venerable St Andrews, although it was originally common ground shared with grazing cattle, horse-riders and linen bleachers. James II banned golf on the links in 1457 as it interfered with archery practice, but 50 years later James IV took up the game, and Charles I was playing golf at Leith when news was brought to him of the Irish rebellion in 1642.

Aerial view of Leith Links.

town, is now home to young professionals and media types, with the slightly tongue-in-cheek promotional slogan 'Leith-sur-Mer'. Fashionable restaurants and up-market apartment blocks seem to be constantly sprouting amid the fine merchant buildings of the past.

THE FOOT OF THE WALK

Catch any of the numerous buses to Leith from across the city centre (check with the driver that it goes down Constitution Street) or take a short taxi ride. Whatever your transport choice, you will pass along wide **Leith Walk**, arriving in the district at 'the foot of the walk', where a statue of Queen Victoria stands in front of a rather soulless shopping centre.

The Queen arrived here in her yacht the *Royal George* in 1842, but put ashore at Granton along the coast. Constitution Street continues northward from the foot of Leith Walk to arrive at the junction with Bernard Street, where on the right are the historic **Leith Assembly Rooms**, closed except for private functions. Constitution Street then approaches **Leith Docks**, evolved from John Rennie's plan in the early 19th century. The Victoria Dock was built in 1851, the Albert Dock in 1869 and the Edinburgh Dock in 1881.

Leith Links

A diversion to the east of Constitution Street along Queen Charlotte Street leads to **Leith Links** ❶, a fairly flat park of interest to lovers of **golf**. The Honourable Company of Edinburgh Golfers established their first clubhouse here in the late 18th

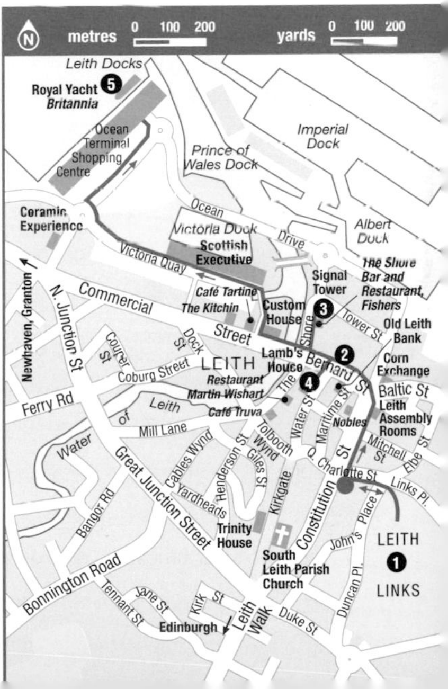

Soft Play

Located on the second floor of the Ocean Terminal shopping centre is the soft play experience Oceanplay (tel: 0131-555 1900; Mon–Fri 9.30am–6pm, Sat–Sun 10am–6pm). This is an ideal place to go with your kids (all ages up to early teens) on a rainy day or when they need to let off some steam.

century, and though the august body is now based at Muirfield on the East Lothian coast, the 13 rules drawn up for the 1774 tournament form the basis of the game played worldwide today. Regrettably there's no course on Leith Links these days, but you will find a small memorial stone in the western section of the park.

BERNARD STREET AND THE SHORE

The former bustling buildings and tenements of **Bernard Street** ❷ and **The Shore** (which transects it) mostly date from the 1770s. A statue of pre-eminent Scottish poet Robert Burns faces Constitution Street, while the former centre of commerce the **Old Leith Bank** lies a block westwards. **Bernard Street Bridge**, which crosses the river to Commercial Street, was originally a drawbridge dating from the early 19th century but was rebuilt in the 1950s.

Old architecture mixes with new along the waterfront.

Fish n Ships sculpture.

Hugging the east bank of the Water of Leith, turn right along restaurant-filled **The Shore** to reach the **Signal Tower** ❸. Now lying above popular restaurant *Fishers* (see page 93), it was built in 1686 and once had a two-storey timber windmill on top of the existing tower, and was only converted to enable flag communication with ships on the Firth of Forth during the Napoleonic Wars. Beyond it, a pedestrian square has been laid in front of the stylish Malmaison hotel, converted from the Victorian Seamen's Mission. The original **King's Wark**, now a pub, was built by James I in 1438 and burnt down at least five times in the four successive centuries.

Take the time to wander along the inland section of The Shore, where a little imagination can envisage the chaotic hubbub of bygone ages. A block eastwards on Water Street is the equally evocative **Lamb's House** ❹, a 17th-century merchant's house, where Mary, Queen of Scots allegedly rested upon her return to Scottish soil in 1561. It has been restored by the

National Trust for Scotland and currently serves as offices.

If you're feeling especially active, you might contemplate walking part of the Water of Leith footpath along the river, which after 2.5 miles (4km) arrives at the end of Warriston Crescent, close to where Route 7 begins.

THE OLD QUAYS AND NEW OCEAN TERMINAL

Across Bernard Street Bridge is the **Leith Custom House**, designed by Robert Reid in 1812 and currently managed by the Scottish Historic Buildings Trust. Nearby, King's Landing is where George IV stepped ashore on his celebrated visit to Edinburgh in 1822. The whole immediate stretch of land between Commercial Street and Victoria Quay is lined with converted warehouses now serving as restaurants for the new affluent Leith class. Following this modern-cobbled road westwards, the purpose-built headquarters of the **Scottish Executive** loom large on the right. Closer to the western end of Commercial Street/Victoria Quay are the Sands where pirates were hanged – so-called 'within the floddis mark' – though the last such execution for piracy took place in 1823, when two foreigners expiated their crime on a gibbet erected opposite the foot of Constitution Street.

Leith has a long tradition of shipbuilding.

Ocean Terminal and Royal Yacht Britannia

Following the road around to the north, the glazed **Ocean Terminal shopping centre** (www.oceanterminal.com; Mon–Fri 10am–8pm, Sat

Ships and Shipbuilding

In the 17th century, Leith established a major reputation for the building of timber vessels, and even Peter the Great of Russia came to learn about shipbuilding before creating his own devastating Baltic fleet. In 1698 the ill-fated Darien Expedition set sail from Leith to colonise a strategic stretch of Central American land for Scotland, but a combination of tropical disease and the Spanish hostility – intent on their own colonial aspirations – coupled with the refusal of Westminster to give assistance, led to the financial ruin of many Scottish families.

Nonetheless, Leith's position was maintained in 1720, when Britain's first dry dock was built here, an advanced construction that didn't escape Scottish-born American renegade Paul Jones, who in 1779 made an abortive attempt to capture the port with a small French squadron displaying American colours. Activity boomed during the Napoleonic Wars, and strong links were forged as the wine trade developed.

The golden age was over, however, as shipbuilding began to change in the 19th century with the introduction of iron hulls. Lacking the necessary deep-water facilities, Leith went rapidly into decline.

10am–7pm, Sun 11am–6pm) affords views over the Forth from its concourses and open-plan restaurants. The huge development was opened in 2001 and provides a great alternative for those who wish to avoid the bustle of the city centre.

Most visitors come here to see the **Royal Yacht *Britannia*** ❺ (tel: 0131-555 5566; www.royalyachtbritannia.co.uk; daily Apr–Sept 9.30am–4.30pm, Oct 9.30am–4pm, Nov–Mar 10am–3.30pm), however, accessed from a second-floor visitor centre within the mall. The Royal Yacht was launched in 1953 and came to rest here in 1998. The visitor centre introduces the 412ft (126m) 'yacht', and the Royal Family's accommodation together with the 240-strong crew's quarters give an insight into life at sea, also assisted by an anecdote-filled audio-guide. If you are returning to Edinburgh centre by bus, Nos. 11 and 22 operates regularly.

LOCAL DIVERSIONS

From Commercial Street and the Ocean Terminal, the coastal road runs 0.75 miles (1.25km) alongside the shore of the Firth of Forth to the former fishing village of **Newhaven**. The community is slightly dilapidated, but the enclosed harbour still sits pretty with its traditional lighthouse on the seaward side. The harbour was built by James IV in the 16th century as a dockyard for his expanding navy. Being determined to create the largest ocean-going vessel of his age, he had *Great Michael* constructed here – the ship was 240ft (73m) long and equipped to carry 300 sailors, 1,000 soldiers and 120 gunners.

Nearer the foot of Leith Walk at Kirkgate, accessed through the far end of the 1960s shopping precinct behind the statue of Queen Victoria, is **Trinity House** (tel: 0131-554 3289; tours by appointment only; free). Built in 1816 for the Trinity Association of Mariners (who have occupied the site since 1555), the house has a magnificent interior and contains paintings, models and rare artefacts relating to Leith's maritime history. The Kirkgate pedestrian walkway (with flats at the north end drawing attention to the contrast between living

The Royal Yacht *Britannia* was launched in 1953.

Leith harbour walls.

standards here and at the gentrified waterfront) replaced a once-thriving street, lined with shops, pubs and a music hall, demolished in the 1960s. The name refers to **South Leith Parish Church**, which still stands opposite Trinity House. The church is Victorian, but was remodelled from the remains of a large 15th-century church, St Mary's, that was partly destroyed during the 1560 Siege of Leith by the Protestant adversaries of Mary of Guise. Stones in the kirkyard date back to this earlier age, remembering merchants, seamen and members of the trade guilds, who built chapels alongside the nave.

Eating Out

Café Tartine
72 Commercial Street; tel: 0131-554 2588; www.cafetartine.co.uk; Mon–Thu 8am–11pm, Fri 8am–1am, Sat 9am–1am, Sun 9am–11pm.
Bright airy space with communal wooden tables, offering a French café menu of freshly made crêpes alongside a tasty croque-monsieur plus moules marinières and surf 'n' turf. ££

Café Truva
77 The Shore; tel: 0131-554 5502; www.cafetruva.com; daily 7am–5pm.
Turkish café right on the Water of Leith, serving a really good-value meze, a choice of wholesome breakfasts and Turkish and traditional coffees. £

Fishers
1 The Shore; tel: 0131-554 5666; www.fishersrestaurants.co.uk; daily noon–10pm.
The original Fishers has a lovely setting underneath the watchtower close to the harbourside. Fish and seafood are predominant, but meats such as venison also feature. Value set menus are available. ££

The Kitchin
78 Commercial Quay; tel: 0131-555 1755; www.thekitchin.com; Tue–Sat noon–2.30pm, 6–10pm.
Aptly named chef Tom Kitchin has won a string of awards including a Michelin star for his restaurant on the Leith waterfront. His philosophy is 'from nature to plate', and his seasonal menus feature dishes such as locally sourced rabbit or veal and exceptional local seafood creations. The ambience is refreshingly relaxed. £££

Nobles
44a Constitution Street; tel: 0131-629 7215; www.noblesbarleith.co.uk; Tue–Sun 10am–11pm, (Sat–Sun closes 1am).
A friendly place with fine ales. Good brunch, lunch and dinner menus make the most of the great Scottish produce on the doorstep. ££

Restaurant Martin Wishart
54 The Shore; tel: 0131-553 3557; www.martin-wishart.co.uk; Tue–Sat noon–1.30pm, 7–9pm.
Martin Wishart's Michelin-starred eponymous restaurant is one of the most highly rated in Scotland. It offers exquisite modern French cuisine using top-quality Scottish ingredients, in a somewhat formal venue. Legendary seafood. £££

The Shore Bar and Restaurant
3 Shore; tel: 0131-553 5080; www.fishersrestaurants.co.uk; daily noon–late.
Popular bar and one-room restaurant offering a small but varied menu that delivers classic British dishes with a modern twist, all to a high quality. ££

The Forth Railway Bridge.

Tour 9

Excursion to Firth of Forth

Dominated by the towering Forth Bridges, the Firth of Forth estuary is the classic Edinburgh out-of-town trip and this 12 mile (19km) route will take up most of a day

From Edinburgh's northern fringes, this tour takes in a few stately homes (of which Hopetoun House is the most impressive) and a walk through historic, affluent Cramond, and includes the possibility of a ferry trip to Inchcolm Island and abbey, with the chance to see puffins, seals and dolphins. Dominated by the giant frame of the Forth Railway Bridge, South Queensferry is a pretty cobbled town on the shoreline, ideal for refreshments.

Most of this tour can be visited on public transport, with regular bus No. 41 (Lothian) from Edinburgh to Lauriston Castle and on to Cramond, and bus No. 43 (Lothian Country) to South Queensferry. A good alternative is to walk the Cramond-Dalmeny-South Queensferry stretch along the coast (see box). Trains also ply the route to South Queensferry – though you'll have to descend the long steps down to Hawes Pier from Dalmeny station above.

Highlights

- Lauriston Castle
- Cramond
- South Queensferry
- The Forth Bridges
- Boat cruise to Inchcolm Island
- Hopetoun House

NORTH TO CRAMOND

Turn off Queensferry Road at Davidson's Mains to arrive at grand **Lauriston Castle** ❶ (2a Cramond Road

Boats moored on the River Almond estuary at Cramond.

Dalmeny Shore Walk

A beautiful path along the shore of the Firth of Forth starts at Cramond, passes through the **Dalmeny Estate** close to Dalmeny House, and finishes at South Queensferry, 4.5 miles (7km) further west. With great views of the estuary across to Fife, you'll also discover medieval towers, ancient woodland and a golf course along the route. At the start, you'll need to cross the River Almond: in 1556 a tiny ferry was established to get across to the estate, but it has long since closed. Despite speculation in the past that the ferry might reopen, there are currently no plans to reinstate it. You can walk around instead, although this involves a diversion of 1.5 miles (2.5km) – follow the path upstream to the **Cramond Brig** and enter via the East Craigie Gate.

South; tel: 0131-336 2060; www.edinburghmuseums.org.uk; guided tour only Apr–Oct Mon–Thu 2pm, Sat–Sun 2pm, 2.30pm, 3pm and 3.30pm, Nov–Mar Sat–Sun 2pm; check website for possible weekday tours Nov–Dec), which resembles more of a stately home than a fortress, with a 16th-century tower once owned by the Napiers of Merchiston and good views across the Firth of Forth. Various owners have since added new sections and refurbished the interior, and the property is now held in trust by the city with a collection of Edwardian furniture and decorative art.

Those familiar with Muriel Spark's 1961 novel *The Prime of Miss Jean Brodie* (or the 1969 film version starring Maggie Smith) will recall the picnics enjoyed by the strong-minded schoolmistress and her girls at **Cramond** ❷, ten minutes' walk or a short bus ride (No. 41) beyond Lauriston Castle. A lovingly restored, 18th-century village on the estuary of the River Almond on the Firth of Forth, it's a great place to get out of the city for a walk.

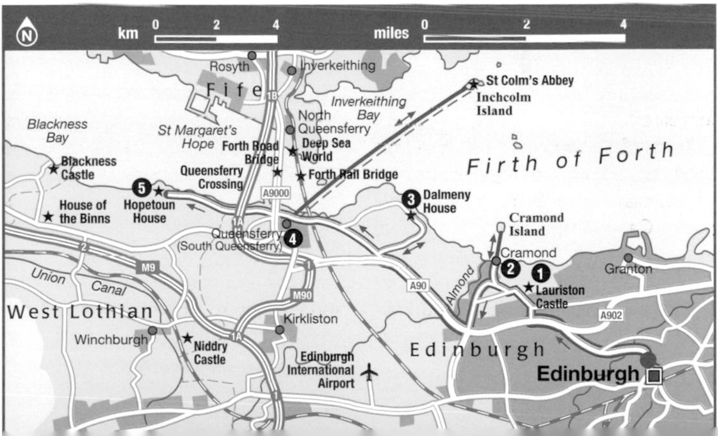

Interesting old tombstones abound in the churchyard of Cramond Kirk.

The name Cramond originates from the Cumbric *Caer Amon* meaning 'Fort on the Almond', though excavations carried out in the 1960s and 1970s indicate that it had previously been a Roman harbour station. The current cruciform church **Cramond Kirk** dates from 1656, but the site was probably used by the early Christians. An interesting find, displayed in the National Museum of Scotland, is a stone carving of a lioness devouring her prey; this piece would have been buried with a wealthy Roman.

Dalmeny House.

Along the Almond to Cramond Island

The finest walk in the area is an amble along the River Almond towards the Firth of Forth, along which you'll spot **Cramond Tower**, a small, 14th-century four-storey keep that served as a summer palace for the bishops of Dunkeld, who occupied the medieval village. These days, somewhat bizarrely, the tower is occupied by a taxidermist (see www.scottish-taxidermy.co.uk), who has painstakingly restored the property with new beams and fireplaces, and uses the ground floor as a gallery for paintings and displays of his numerous stuffed animals.

In the 18th century, the Almond became famous for being the first place to commercially produce Scottish crude steel with four local mills – but today the river has become a popular summer yachting resort for a wealthy class of Scots and has a lively social life. Nearby, at low tide, you can walk across the causeway to the nature reserve of **Cramond Island**, though it's essential to take note of incoming tide times (given on the causeway's noticeboard) to avoid being stranded.

The causeway to Cramond Island.

DALMENY HOUSE

Just south of Cramond, the Queensferry Road leads to South Queensferry, and 2 miles (3.5km) along its course are the gates of **Dalmeny House** ❸ (tel: 0131-331 1888; www.dalmeny.co.uk; June–July Sun–Wed by tour only 2.15pm and 3.30pm), home of the earls of Rosebery.

Designed in 1815 by English architect William Wilkins, it was the first Tudor Gothic Revival house in Scotland, though the surrounding estate goes back much further; together with Barnbougle Castle, a Norman keep situated on the shores of the Firth of Forth, it was acquired by the Primrose family in 1662. The story goes that the Third Earl, when rising from dinner at Barnbougle, was bowled over by a large wave of water and decided at once to build a larger, safer residence.

The Fifth Earl, Lord Rosebery (British prime minister 1894–95), married a Rothschild heiress, and many of the remarkable treasures on display at Dalmeny come from their home at Mentmore, England, sold in 1977. These include colourful tapestries designed by Goya for the Spanish royal residences, a selection of fine Louis XV French furniture and a Napoleon Room, which is filled with the Fifth Earl's collection of memorabilia belonging to the Emperor.

SOUTH QUEENSFERRY

Two miles beyond Dalmeny House on the A90, the town of **South Queensferry** ❹ crouches under the shadow of the rusty red **Forth Railway Bridge**, completed in 1890 with three giant steel humps – a total length over the Forth estuary of 6,156ft (1,876m). It opened up the east coast rail line to Perth, Inverness

Aerial view of the Queensferry Crossing and the Forth Road Bridge.

Queensferry Crossing

Opened in August 2017, this project has changed the face of the Firth of Forth, and created a new river landscape. The Queensferry Crossing and extension to the M90 was designed to ease the traffic flow, although this has had limited success and various schemes are to be implemented to try and improve the flow. At 1.7 miles (2.7km) the impressive structure is the longest three-tower cable-stayed bridge in the world, and its construction makes it ultra-strong. The old bridge, however, still plays its part, being designated for walkers, cyclists and public transport.

Close encounter in the underwater viewing tunnel.

Deep Sea World

Just across the Forth Road Bridge at North Queensferry is Scotland's largest aquarium, Deep Sea World (tel: 01383-411 880; www.deepseaworld.com; Mon–Fri 10am–5pm, Sat–Sun 10am–6pm), which will appeal as much to adults as children, with its diver's eye-view of the deep from a 367ft (112m) -long viewing tunnel alongside recreations of ecosystems from the Amazon and Lake Malawi.

and Aberdeen, while the less impressive **Forth Road Bridge** opened in 1964 to carry traffic along its suspended frame. The impressive Queensferry Crossing road bridge to the west opened in 2017 (see box).

An eye-catching cobbled main street reveals numerous old shops and houses from the 17th and 18th centuries, while its one attraction of significance, the **Queensferry Museum** (53 High Street; tel: 0131-331 5545; www.edinburghmuseums.org.uk; daily 10am–1pm, 2.15–5pm; free) tells the story of the place and its people. The town was originally known as 'the Queen's Ferry' in honour of saintly Queen Margaret, wife of Malcolm Canmore, who encouraged pilgrims in the 11th century to use the ferry crossing to visit the shrine of St Andrew in Fife by granting them free passage.

If you're intrigued as to what's on the other side of the bridges, an easy diversion from here by rail from Dalmeny station is southern **Fife**, with numerous historic villages and towns. Most notably, Dunfermline is the burial place of Robert the Bruce, and Culross, another royal burgh, is a small village with a number of 16th- and 17th-century sites restored and managed by the National Trust for Scotland.

The Forth Railway Bridge.

Sphinx statue in the gardens of Hopetoun House.

Island Cruise

In fine weather, the best panoramas of the Firth of Forth can be had from a downriver cruise on the *Maid of the Forth* (tel: 0131-331 5000; www.maidoftheforth.co.uk; times vary, see website for sailings), departing from the Hawes Pier to the island of **Inchcolm** (3-hour round trip), with regular sightings of seals, dolphins, puffins, oyster catchers, cormorants and fulmars. Ashore, you can visit the intriguing ruin of **St Colm's Abbey** (founded in 1123), mentioned in Shakespeare's *Macbeth*.

HOPETOUN HOUSE

To the west of South Queensferry is **Hopetoun House** ❺ (tel: 0131-331 2451; www.hopetoun.co.uk; Apr–Sept daily 10.30am–5pm), the impressive family home of the earls and marquesses of Linlithgow. The first mansion was designed by Sir William Bruce and built in 1699, but William Adam enlarged it in 1721, adding a magnificent facade, colonnades and state apartments, work continued after his death by his sons John, Robert and James. Most of the original 18th-century furniture and wall coverings can still be seen, as well as opulent gilding and fine classical motifs. Visitors can wander at leisure in the large, delightful grounds, full of rare specimen trees, well-attended red deer parkland and woodland walks.

Eating Out

Cramond

Cramond Falls Café

10 School Brae; tel: 0131-312 8408; daily 10am–4pm (Sat until 4.30pm).

Attractively set by the river, Cramond offers homemade cakes, sandwiches, special dishes of the day and all-day breakfasts. £

South Queensferry

The Boathouse

22 High Street; tel: 0131-331 5429; www.theboathouse-sq.co.uk; daily noon–9pm.

Part delicatessen, part wine bar, part seafood restaurant, and the views of the Forth Railway Bridge don't get any better from the mainland than from here. You'll find good fresh fish, seafood and meat choices, too. ££

Hawes Inn

7 Newhalls Road, South Queensferry; tel: 0131-331 1990; daily noon–11pm.

Despite now being part of a chain, this place is still somewhere that should not be missed. Dating from 1683, it was used by Robert Louis Stevenson in *Kidnapped* for the fictional meeting between Uncle Ebenezer and the Captain of the brig *Covenant*. ££

Picnic Coffee Shop

5 Mid Terrace; tel: 0131-331 1346; www.picniccoffeeshop.com; Mon–Sat 9am–5pm, Sun 10am–5pm.

This is a friendly small café serving locals and visitors alike. Does sandwiches, soups and more, with both Scottish and Italian influences. £

Linlithgow Palace.

Tour 10

Excursion to Edinburgh Zoo, Linlithgow and Falkirk

This day-long 25 mile (40km) round-trip takes you due west of Edinburgh to the stunning lakeside setting of Linlithgow Palace, the city zoo, and out to the Falkirk Wheel

The two major destinations along this route – Linlithgow, birthplace of Mary, Queen of Scots, and the 21st-century engineering marvel that is the Falkirk Wheel – can both be visited by train from Edinburgh Waverley (take any stopping train going to Glasgow Queen Street station). For the Falkirk Wheel, you'll need to alight at Falkirk High train station and either walk the 2.5 miles (4km) along the beautiful canal towpath, or use the taxi services available outside the station.

An alternative is to rent bicycles in Edinburgh, take them by train to Linlithgow and then cycle the 10 miles (16km) onwards to Falkirk along the canal.

Highlights

- Corstorphine and Edinburgh Zoo
- Linlithgow Palace
- Falkirk Wheel

WEST TO CORSTORPHINE HILL

Just over a mile (2km) from Edinburgh's Haymarket station on the A8 Corstorphine Road (bus No. 12, 26 or 31) and situated on 70 acres (28 hectares) of landscaped hillside, is **Edinburgh Zoo** ❶ (tel: 0131-334 9171; www.edinburghzoo.org.uk; daily Apr–Sept 10am–6pm, Oct and Mar until 5pm, Nov–Feb until 4.30pm). It is one

Don't miss the penguin parade at Edinburgh Zoo.

Penguin Pen

The first penguins to arrive at Edinburgh Zoo did so courtesy of the Leith-based whaling company, Christian Salveson & Co, which in 1908 set up a Leith Harbour on the bleak coastline of South Georgia in the Antarctic. By 1911 they had become the biggest whaling company in the world, and, though they quit the business when the price of whale oil fell in the 1960s, the zoo is still renowned for its penguins.

of Britain's largest, featuring numerous animals, but most popular for its penguins and its giant pandas Tian Tian (Sweetie) and Yang Guang (Sunshine).

Corstorphine Hill, which rises 530ft (162m) above the zoo, features **Clermiston Tower**, built in 1871 to mark the centenary of Sir Walter Scott's birth, and nearby **Corstorphine** village is famous for the **Corstorphine Sycamore**, a botanical sub-species, of which only the stump unfortunately remains (it was once 55ft/17m high). The 'White Lady of Corstorphine', said to be the ghostly mistress of a 17th-century local landowner, is sometimes seen to take a turn around where the tree once flourished. A little further westwards (exit from the Newbridge roundabout on the M9) immediately beyond Edinburgh airport, you'll gain sight of semi-ruined **Niddry Castle**, a tall late 15th-century tower now surrounded by a golf course. It was to here in 1568 that Mary, Queen of Scots fled following her escape from imprisonment in Loch Leven castle.

LINLITHGOW

Many of the buildings in the historic royal burgh of **Linlithgow** ❷, one of the finest destinations outside of the city, have been restored by the National Trust for Scotland. **St Michael's Parish Church** (daily), close to the palace and dating from the 15th century, is listed as one of the finest medieval churches in Scotland – although the 'crown of thorns' spire was added in

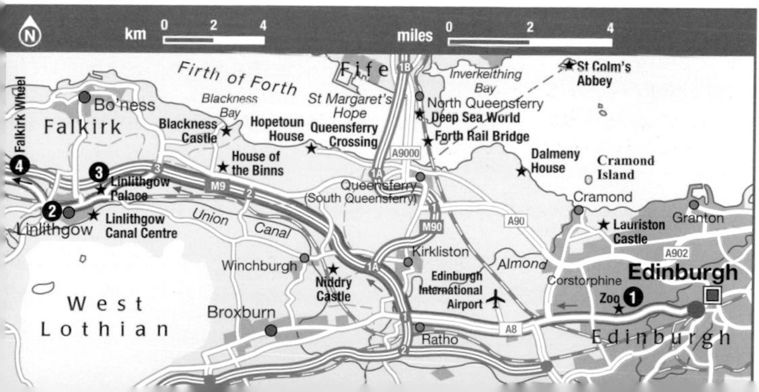

Hamlet's Castle

On a promontory on the coast just north of Linlithgow stands **Blackness Castle** (tel: 01506-834 807; www.historicenvironment.scot; Apr–Sept daily 9.30am–5.30pm, Oct–Mar Sat–Wed 10am–4pm), referred to as 'the ship that never sailed', as from the sea it looks like a ship that has run aground. Built in the 15th century by the Earl of Caithness, it was used by King James V as a state prison, armaments depot and stronghold against Henry VIII, until it was sacked by Oliver Cromwell. The dramatically sited fortress was used as a location for the 1990 film version of *Hamlet*, starring Mel Gibson. To get here, take a bus (First Scotland East No. F49) from Linlithgow Cross on the High Street to Blackness, from where it's a short walk.

1964. Edward I of England used Linlithgow as a base for his attack on Stirling, but the English garrison was taken by Scottish soldiers smuggled inside the walls in a hay wagon. Find out more about the town at the **Linlithgow Museum** on the High Street (check www.visitscotland.com for further details; free), opening in 2019.

Meercats at Edinburgh Zoo.

The **Linlithgow Canal Centre** (tel: 01506-671 215; www.lucs.org.uk; Easter–Sept Sat–Sun 1–4.30pm, also July–mid-Aug Mon–Fri 2–4pm; free), located on the hill above the train station, houses records, photographs and relics relating to the Union Canal, which officially closed in 1965. The canal connected with Lock 16 of the Forth and Clyde Canal at Falkirk, making it possible to sail all the way from Edinburgh to Glasgow, and, although commercial traffic no longer plies its course, frequent short trips depart from the Centre and on weekends (confirm in advance) a boat leaves at 2pm for a 2.5-hour trip to the spectacular **Avon Viaduct**, the longest in Scotland. Boats also occasionally depart for the Falkirk Wheel, met by a bus for the journey to Linlithgow.

Linlithgow Palace

With its dramatic and inordinately picturesque lakeside setting, **Linlithgow Palace** ❸ (tel: 01506-842 896; www.historicenvironment.scot; daily Apr–Sept 9.30am–5.30pm, Oct–Mar 10am–4pm) is one of the highlights of a visit to the region.

James I built a palace here in 1425 – though numerous additions were made later – and both James V (1512) and his daughter Mary, Queen of Scots (1542) were born here. The future Charles I was brought up at Linlithgow with his brother and sister, before his father inherited the throne of England and the family moved to London. Charles returned briefly in 1633, and Oliver Cromwell wintered here during his 1650 punitive trip to Scotland, but after that the palace was largely abandoned until being set on fire following Bonnie Prince Charlie's retreat from England. What remain

Blackness Castle was the setting for Franco Zeffirelli's 1990 movie *Hamlet*.

are extensive, partially restored ruins, and in summer, regular special events including Scottish dancing or jousting take place in the palace courtyard.

FALKIRK WHEEL

The remarkable **Falkirk Wheel** ❹ (Lime Road, Tamfourhill, Falkirk; tel: 08700-500 208; www.scottishcanals.co.uk/falkirk-wheel; daily 10am–5.30pm, see website for winter opening; visitor centre free, charge for boat trip) opened in 2003 as the world's first rotating boatlift, linking the Forth and Clyde and the Union canals, which in turn link Edinburgh with Glasgow along one waterway. A remarkable cantilever construction, the lift amazingly uses the power of just seven electric kettles to lift tonnes of steel 115ft (35m) to the canal above.

Board an excursion boat (every 40 mins) on the Forth and Clyde Canal outside the **Visitor Centre**, where it soon enters the Wheel's lower gondola. Arriving above, it sails along a short aqueduct and enters into the upper (Union) canal. By car, the A803 runs between Linlithgow and Falkirk, while the M9 runs direct to Edinburgh.

The Falkirk Wheel.

Eating Out

Linlithgow

Barleo

50 High Street; tel: 01506-846 667; www.barleo.co.uk; Mon–Fri noon–2.30pm, 5–10pm, Fri–Sat noon–11pm, Sun noon–10pm.
A smart Italian wood-panelled restaurant, serving good thin-crust pizzas, pasta and other Italian dishes using top-quality ingredients. ££

So Strawberry Café

3 The Cross; tel: 01506-843 3333; Mon–Sat 9am–4.30pm, Sun 10am–4.30pm.
Perfectly placed by the entrance to Linlithgow Castle, this cosy little café with outside tables is great for breakfast, coffee and home-made cake, light lunch or afternoon tea. £

The Pentland Hills.

Tour 11

Excursion South to Roslin and Pentland Hills

South of Edinburgh, hidden pretty suburban areas meander into gorgeous rural settings in the Braid and Pentland Hills. Driving, this 15-mile (24km) tour can take over half a day

If travelling by bus, take No. 15 from Princes Street, Lothian Road or Tollcross to get to Morningside, the Royal Observatory and onwards to the ski centre and Roslin (also bus No. 37) – though to reach Currie, Balerno and Colinton you'll need to retrace steps back to Princes Street and catch No. 44 via Haymarket. Another alternative is to follow the more adventurous **Water of Leith Walkway**, which curves around from the New Town into southwest Edinburgh, eventually passing through dimly lit **Colinton Tunnel,** before taking in fine homes in the well-heeled suburbs and country estates close to Currie and Balerno.

Highlights

- Royal Observatory and Braid Hills
- Pentland Hills Regional Park
- Rosslyn Chapel
- Roslin Glen Country Park
- Currie
- Balerno

SOUTH TO BRAID HILLS

Heading southwards from the road junction of **Tollcross** (bus No. 15) to the west of the **Meadows,** the residential areas of **Merchiston** and then **Morningside** meander south-wards along the Morningside and Comiston roads (A702). The latter

Walkers on Blackford Hill.

district is a popular residential area of Edinburgh, as much celebrated for its refined variation of the Scottish accent as it is teased by Scottish comics for the prim and proper way of the '*Morningside ladies*' (ladies who lunch). To the west of the district, where Colinton Road meets the Burghmuirhead, four churches, one on each corner, welcome you at a junction known as 'Holy Corner'.

Just to the east of Morningside, **Blackford Hill** forms a 100-acre (40-hectare) country park and nature reserve along the **Hermitage of Braid**, an estate with a castellated mansion built in the 18th century, now containing a visitor centre (tel: 0131-529 2416; www.fohb.org; Mon–Fri 9am–4pm) with displays on local ecology and reached from the Braid Road. After the area was bought by the city in 1889, a section was given over to a golf course, and another to the **Royal Observatory** ❶ (tel: 0131-668 8404; www.roe.ac.uk; bus No. 41 from city centre), an internationally recognised institution in astronomical observation. Group tours are available by appointment, and occasional public night-time stargazing sessions are also run here. Close to the complex, the **Harrison Arch** honours a former Lord Provost of Edinburgh who secured public access to the hill.

The Braid Hills

There are fine walks in the **Braid Hills,** which range from here southwards to the Pentland Hills, and across the city from Comiston to Liberton. Blackford and Braid are both included among the 'seven hills of Edinburgh', along with more centrally sited Castle Hill, Calton Hill, Arthur's Seat (the highest), and, to the west, Corstorphine Hill and West Craiglockhart Hill. In the past, fireworks have been simultaneously launched from the Braid Hills at midnight on Hogmanay (31 Dec).

To the southeast is **Liberton**, a 'village' on a hill with a fine parish church. The University of Edinburgh's College of Science and Engineering is here, at the King's Buildings on West Mains Road. The village name may be a corruption of Lepertown, after a leper hospital that once stood here.

PENTLAND HILLS

Continuing out of town on the A702, you cross over the City of Edinburgh Bypass just after subur-

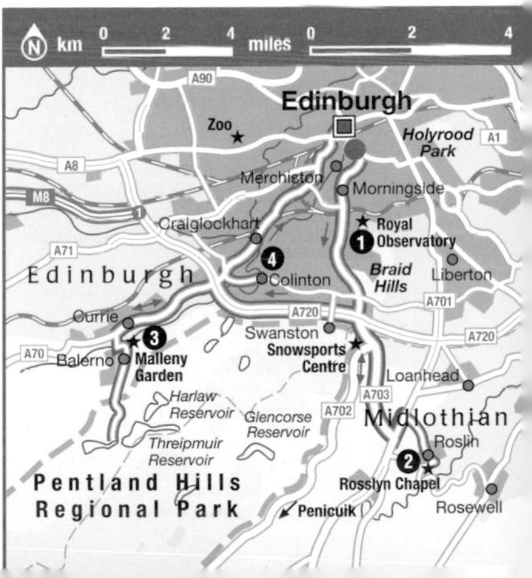

This scenery of low hills is perfect for amateur walkers.

ban Fairmilehead. Close to the bypass but set in splendid isolation southwest is **Swanston,** a cluster of 17th-century whitewashed cottages once a summer home of Robert Louis Stevenson, where he conceived and wrote his early work. From here the road ascends into the northern slopes of the **Pentland Hills**, past the **Snowsports Centre** at Hillend, Europe's longest artificial ski slope (daily year round), where trails also lead off into the hills. At night, when the slope is lit up against the dark sky, it is said to resemble 'a stairway to God'.

Rosslyn Chapel.

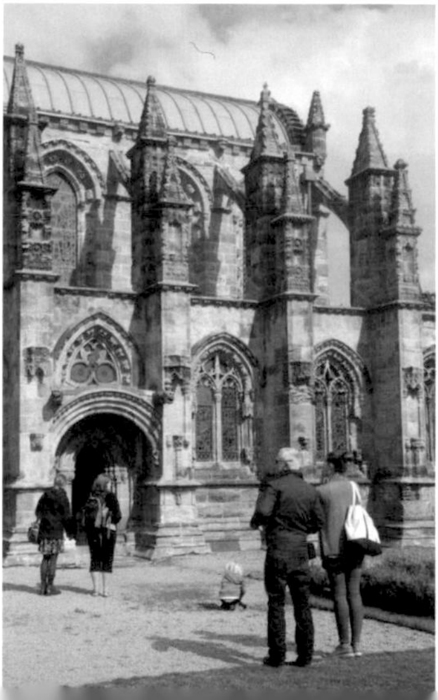

Skirting the south of Edinburgh, the **Pentland Hills Regional Park** (tel: 0131-529 2401; www.pentlandhills.org) provides ample space for hiking – including around 62 miles (100km) of waymarked paths – and other outdoor activities across windswept, heather-strewn moorland. Three miles (5km) beyond the Snowsports Centre, the Flotterstone Visitor Centre (Mon–Fri 9.30am–4pm, Sat–Sun 10am–4pm) is a small facility with maps, ideas for walking routes and information on weather and the local environment. A further information centre is located at **Harlaw** (Mon–Fri 11am–3.30pm, Sat–Sun 11.30am–3pm) on the other side of the hills beyond Balerno. Nearby, **Harlaw Reservoir** and **Threipmuir Reservoir** are both popular venues for country walks.

ROSLIN

Branch left just after the Snowsports Centre to join the A701 towards Penicuik (also bus No. 15), where signs lead to **Roslin**, a former mining village that was once home to the **Roslin Institute Research Centre**, where Dolly, the first cloned sheep, was created.

Another claim to fame, however, is the beautiful **Rosslyn Chapel** ❷ (tel: 0131-440 2159; www.rosslynchapel.com; Mon–Sat 9.30am–5pm (until 6pm Jun–Aug), Sun noon–4.45pm, children free), also known as the Collegiate Church of St Michael.

The interior of the church, which was constructed in 1446, is decorated with remarkable carvings, notably elaborate columns such as the flower-covered **Apprentice Pillar**, so called because it was carved by an apprentice stone-mason during the absence of his master – the latter consequently killed the apprentice with a mallet on seeing the phenomenal work. Links between the chapel, its owners the St Clairs and the Knights Templar, are well documented, not least in the book and film of *The Da Vinci Code* – though Walter Scott's *Marmion* also recalls that the Order are buried in full armour beneath the chapel, having fled to Scotland from Europe during the 12th-century reign of David I.

The Pentland Hills

A stunning stretch of scenic hills, lowland brooks and rich wildlife conservation area, the Pentland Hills Regional Park is an oasis of untamed tranquillity within easy reach of Edinburgh. It is home to fauna such as roe deer, brown hare, stoats and water voles, and avifauna including oystercatchers, red shank and meadow pipits. The best places to begin a walk are at the car park beside the Flotterstone Inn or from the Snowsports Centre, both on the east side of the hills off the A702. From Flotterstone, a board shows the many footpaths and rangers arrange guided walks and events (tel: 0131-529 2401). The highest point is Scald Law, which rises to 1,900ft (579m).

Threipmuir Reservoir.

Coachloads of visitors affect the experience of a visit here, but if caught at a quiet time the beauty of the stonework is unquestionable.

Accessed from a path below the chapel are the beautiful woodlands of **Roslin Glen Country Park** on the banks of the River North Esk. **Rosslyn Castle**, built by Henry Sinclair, Earl of Orkney, in the 14th century, is a short distance from the chapel, dropping dramatically down the cliff-face of a rocky promontory that loops around it on three sides. Extensions in the 15th century included the cutting of a deep gorge and addition of a drawbridge, but, now owned by the Earl of Rosslyn, the castle is partly converted into holiday homes. A lovely 3-mile (5km) walk leads from here along the banks of the river to Penicuik, where you can look out for roe deer, kingfishers and freshwater trout.

CURRIE, BALERNO AND COLINTON

On the western side of the Pentland Hills, and, if you are driving, accessed on the A70 two junctions along the city bypass from Fairmilehead, **Currie** takes its name from the Celtic *curagh* (a hollow) or the Roman *coria* (a meeting place), its two halves united by the 600-year-old **Currie Bridge**. The present **Currie Kirk** dates from 1784 and has further connections with the Knights Templar, their stones lying in its graveyard.

Children explore Malleny Garden.

Beyond Currie, tucked below the A70 at the highest workable stretch of the **Water of Leith** river before it disappears into its source in the Pentland Hills, is pretty **Balerno**, with numerous neat gardens surrounding the river. Nearby, on a tributary of the Water of Leith by Bavelaw Burn, is the **Malleny Garden** ❸ (tel: 0131-665 1546; www.nts.org.uk;

Enjoying an ice cream in the shadow of the Forth Bridge.

Flower borders at Malleny Garden.

daily 10am–dusk), a delightful 3-acre (1.2-hectare) walled garden with 400-year-old yew trees and old-fashioned roses. The early 17th-century mansion next door is not available to visit, but there is also extensive woodland for a peaceful stroll.

Heading northeastwards on the A70 back into Edinburgh, **Colinton** ❹ began as a milling settlement neatly tucked into a sandstone gorge formed by the Water of Leith. The first traces of a village at Colinton appeared in 1095, when a ford across the river was an important crossing point over the steep river valley, but most associations with the village are now drawn from the 17th century, when the Covenanting Army, which had risen up in defiance of Charles II's imposition of the Episcopalian religion on Scotland, was roundly defeated by General Tam Dalyell nearby in the Pentland Hills.

The **Covenanters' Monument** stands near Redford House in Colinton, now in the British Army's Redford Barracks and Dreghorn Camp.

The intricate Apprentice Pillar in Rosslyn Chapel.

Eating Out

Near Penicuik

Flotterstone Inn

Milton Bridge (A702 Biggar Road); tel: 01968-673 717; www.flotterstoneinn.com; daily lunch and dinner.

Popular with walkers coming in from the Pentland Hills, this traditional Scottish pub serves a wide menu of good food in its restaurant. Bar menu available noon–late. ££

Marchmont

The Rabbit Hole

11 Roseneath Street; tel: 0131-229 7953; www.therabbitholerestaurant.com; Tue–Sat lunch and dinner.

Just south of the Meadows (on your way out or back into Edinburgh), this small neighbourhood restaurant is a cut above many in the city and far off the tourist trail. ££

Portobello Beach.

Tour 12

Excursion East along the Coast

Heading east and following the coast, this 11-mile (18km) half-day route passes through traditional seaside towns, before heading inland to the Scottish Mining Museum

Portobello is just a short ride on the No. 26 bus from Princes Street. A car is not needed to visit Musselburgh and Prestonpans, as trains run along the east coast regularly from Waverley Station. The North British Railway first established this route in 1850, assuring the popularity of the seaside towns as day-trip and holiday destinations in the Victorian age. Inland, and accessible by buses No. 29 or 33 from Princes Street, the Scottish Mining Museum is an atmospheric option for learning more about Edinburgh's industrial heritage – a coal industry that covered most of the coastal area east of the city.

Highlights

- Portobello and Musselburgh
- Scottish Mining Museum
- Prestonpans

THE EASTERN COAST

Heading east from the city centre along London Road, you pass **Meadowbank Sports Stadium**, erected for the 1970 Commonwealth Games; the stadium closed in 2017 for redevelopment and is due to reopen in 2020. Beyond, on the coast (and also accessed from Leith) is **Portobello** ❶, which reputedly was given its name by a seafarer who had taken part in the capture of Puerto Bello in Panama in 1739. It acquired burgh status on being amalgamated with Edinburgh in 1896, and by then it had become a popular and slightly glamorous residential and

Beaches, Mines and Flumes

A great day out for adventurous youngsters is to explore the Scottish Mining Museum at Newtongrange, with its eerie atmosphere and interactive museums, followed – in the warm summer days – by a trip to sandy Portobello Beach, a diverting seaside excursion that's been a tradition for beach-loving Scots for around two centuries, for an ice cream on the sands.

Scottish Mining Museum.

holiday resort – Sir Harry Lauder, the great music-hall star of the early 20th century, was born in a cottage here in 1870. Though the later 20th century saw Portobello fall from grace, as overseas travel took off, various attempts have been made to restore its declining appeal, with large quantities of sand imported, and, more recently, the construction of upmarket apartments offering desirable, cheaper living away from the city centre.

On warm summer days, Portobello still attracts thousands of people, however, and the faded, old-fashioned seaside promenade has a certain charm, with good British seaside food served and windy walks an appealing option along the sand. Also located here is one of Britain's few remaining Victorian **Turkish Baths**, located in the Portobello Swim Centre (57 The Promenade; tel: 0131-669 6888), tiled in Turkish style and with four rooms of varying temperatures.

Musselburgh

At the mouth of the River Esk, **Musselburgh** ❷ was named after a bank of mussels in the 13th century, and earned a reputation as 'the Honest Toun', when the inhabitants rejected a reward for honouring the body of the Earl of Moray, who died here in 1332. Flat and national hunt racing takes place regularly on **Musselburgh Racecourse** on the outskirts of the town as the road travels around the coast towards Prestonpans.

A hermitage and chapel here dedicated to Our Lady of Loretto dates from the early 16th century, and was a place of pilgrimage for the sick. The name was later taken by **Loretto School**, which has its grounds and houses within the town – one of these, **Pinkie House**, dates from the 16th century. Nearby is the striking and impressive facade of stately home **Newhailes House** (Newhailes Road; tel: 0131-653 5599; www.nts.org.uk; Apr–

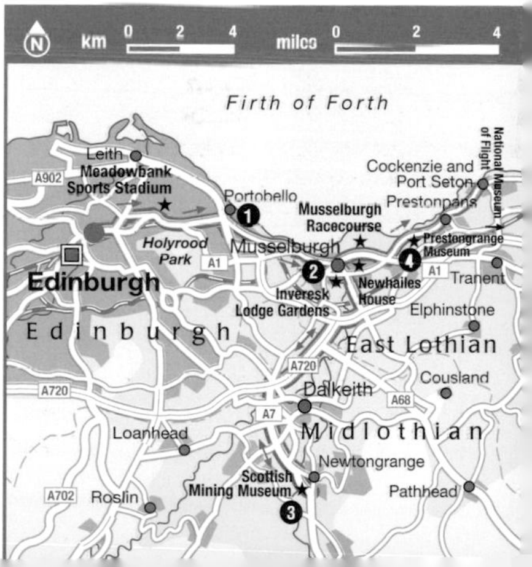

Newhailes House, Musselburgh.

Sept Thu–Mon house: noon–3.30pm by guided tour only, daily July–Aug), the home of Lord Hailes at the time of Dr Samuel Johnson's 1773 tour of Scotland. Built by James Smith in 1686 and added to in the early 1700s, it has a high-quality rococo interior with period paintings and furniture, a fine library and landscaped grounds that retain their 18th-century design. Tours of the property last for 1.25 hours.

Adjoining Musselburgh in easy walking distance to the south, **Inveresk** is a pretty village of garden dwellings, which has been conserved through the efforts of the Inveresk Preservation Society and the National Trust for Scotland. The latter owns **Inveresk Lodge Gardens** (24 Inveresk Village; www.nts.org.uk; daily 10am–5pm or dusk), a delightful terraced garden with wooden areas and an attractive glasshouse featuring rare plants.

Coalface, Scottish Mining Museum.

SCOTTISH MINING MUSEUM

A worthwhile detour 6 miles (10km) inland from the coast at Musselburgh south of Dalkeith, is to **Newtongrange**, one of the best-preserved Victorian mining villages in Scotland.

Located on the A7 3miles (5km) south of the city bypass, it is home to the acclaimed **Scottish Mining Museum** ❸ (tel: 0131-663 7519; www.nationalminingmuseum.com; daily 10am–5pm, until 4pm in winter; by bus take the No. 29 or 33 from the South Bridge or Princes Street), a fascinating and well-presented attraction. It includes a tour of the Lady Victoria Colliery (which closed as a working concern in 1981) led by former miners, and also features 'A Race Apart', where you can find out exactly what it was like to be a miner in the pit. An intensely atmospheric experience, the tour appeals to children and adults, and includes exhibitions on the stories of both coal and Scottish mining communities.

PRESTONPANS AND PRESTONGRANGE

Numerous small towns and pretty villages dot the coast road east of Musselburgh, and the first, **Prestonpans**, though not especially attractive, is historically interesting. In the 12th century monks from Newbattle Abbey started up a salt-panning industry here, though eternal fame was ensured centuries later in 1745, when Prince Charles Edward Stuart (Bonnie Prince Charlie) defeated the English government army led by General John Cope in a famous Jacobite victory. East of the town, a cairn commemorates this **Battle of Prestonpans**, and on its anniversary each 21 September, a

Mural, Prestonpans.

small group of die-hard historians walk to remember the date. In the 18th and 19th centuries Prestonpans was home to no fewer than 16 breweries, at a time when ales were the only safe drink across most of urban Scotland, leading to endemic alcoholism.

East of here, you can walk to **Cockenzie**, formerly a thriving fishing village, but more recently known for its iconic power station with twin towers, which was made the national headlines when it was demolished in September 2015, changing the view of the East Lothian skyline. Adjacent is **Port Seton**, a family holiday resort with a good beach, camping facilities and safe bathing.

Prestongrange Museum

One and a half miles (2.5km) south-west of Prestonpans is a former colliery site with 800 years of mining history, now turned into the **Prestongrange Museum** ❹ (Morison's Haven, Prestonpans; tel: 0131-653 2904; Apr–Sept daily 11.30am–4.30pm; free). The highlight of the guided tour (charge) is the Cornish beam engine that pumped water out of the mine, though there are also brick and glass works, kilns, and a Visitor Centre containing temporary exhibitions on various local industries.

A 20-minute drive east, off the A1, is the **National Museum of Flight** (East Fortune Airfield; tel: 0300-123 6789; www.nms.ac.uk; Apr–Oct daily 10am–5pm, Nov–Mar Sat–Sun 10am–4pm), where you can board Concorde and a Boeing 707.

Eating Out

Portobello

Butternut Squash
10 Bath Street; tel: 07843-013445; www.butternutportobello.co.uk; Mon–Thu 9am–5pm, Fri–Sat 9am–11pm, Sun 10am–5pm.
Located between the High Street and the Promenade, this good-value small restaurant is open daily for breakfast and lunch, and for dinner (££) on Friday and Saturday, when you can bring your own wine. £

Musselburgh

S Luca
32–38 High Street; tel: 0131-665 2237; www.s-luca.co.uk; daily 9am–10pm (Sun from 10am).
A legendary Scottish-Italian ice cream maker, whose café here also serves light lunches, teas and coffees, with a selection of ice cream cakes and a famous knickerbocker glory. £

View of Edinburgh Castle from Blackford Hill.

Path leading to Threipmuir Reservoir.

Travel Tips

Active Pursuits

There's no excuse not to get active in Edinburgh. With hills right in the city centre and a host of easily accessible activities, the city's got it all. For starters, a striking 822ft (250m) hill, Arthur's Seat, lies close to the middle of the city, and, looking up at it, most people at least wonder what the view's like from the top. If steeply uphill is too strenuous, then perhaps try a gentle cycle ride along the Union Canal towpath, or a few miles' stroll along the Water of Leith river walkway. In Muirhouse and Gullane – among others – the surrounding region has some of the most famous golf courses in the world, and there are also renowned climbing and dry-skiing centres.

HILL WALKING

You don't have to move far from your hotel for an active stay in the city. Calton Hill, Blackford Hill and, above all, the Highland-esque Arthur's Seat and neighbouring Salisbury Crags, rising up from behind Holyrood Palace, offer stupendous city views and local opportunities to get legs moving. The Pentland Hills (tel: 0131-529 2401; www.pentlandhills.org), rising steeply from the southern fringes of Edinburgh provide delightful hill walking, and, constantly changing with the seasons, they offer a wild, often barren landscape retreat from the city.

For guided hill walking and hiking tours, or, if you want to go further afield into the Scottish Highlands, check out www.walkaboutscotland.com. Wherever you end up walking, remember that the weather can change very rapidly in Scotland, so take appropriate equipment, clothing and water, and always tell someone where you are going and what time you expect to be back, even if you are in a group.

Cruise or cycle your way to the Falkirk Wheel.

CYCLING

Cycling is an excellent way to explore the leafy Edinburgh suburbs and parks, and in parts of the city there are cycle lanes thanks to campaign groups such as Spokes (tel: 0131-313 2114; www.spokes.org.uk), who publish a map of Edinburgh cycle routes, available from many cycle shops and bookshops.

Perhaps the best opportunity to explore the surrounding countryside is to cycle along the towpath beside the Union Canal, which weaves its way westwards through rolling hills and dramatic gullies from Edinburgh to Falkirk. You can start your ride west of the Castle at Fountainbridge, though for the most enjoyable section put your bike on a train (check with the ticket office at Waverley station) and cycle from Linlithgow to Falkirk, where you'll pass a grand viaduct and finish at engineering wonder the Falkirk Wheel.

Adventure for Kids

Kids will love the **climbing wall** at the Edinburgh International Climbing Arena (EICA; tel: 0131-333 6333; daily). At over a staggering 650ft (200m), this climbing wall was converted from a former quarry, making it the biggest such facility in Europe. There are taster sessions for those who have never climbed before. Under a glass roof, a safe yet hair-raising **aerial assault course** provides further amusement, and there's a soft play area for little ones.

GOLF

Golf is known to have originated in Edinburgh close to Leith docks, so it is not surprising that the capital is well provided with courses. Over 60 golf courses are within one hour's drive of the city, including Muirfield, Gullane, North Berwick and Dunbar. There are various golf passes giving discounted access to courses across Scotland, including those in the immediate city environs. For details on passes and more, visit www.visitscotland.com and follow the links to golf.

The best public-access municipal courses are the two at the Braid Hills (tel: 0131-658 1111; www.braidhillsgolf.co.uk), though you might also consider Carrick Knowe (tel: 0131-

Edinburgh International Climbing Arena.

Fishing on Threipmuir Reservoir.

337 2217; www.carrickknowegolf club.co.uk), Craigentinny (tel: 0131-554 7501), Portobello (nine holes; tel: 0131-669 4361) and Silverknowes (tel: 0131-336 3843; www.silver knowesgc.scot). For Pitch and Putt look no further than Bruntsfield Short Hole Golf Club at the Meadows just south of the Old Town (tel: 0131-445 2705; www.bruntsfieldshortholegolf club.co.uk).

At historic Gullane, east of Edinburgh, a **Heritage of Golf Museum** (viewing by arrangement, tel: 01620-842 742; www.heritageofgolf.org), on West Links Road tells the story of golf's development down the centuries.

Scotland v Italy at Murrayfield Stadium.

HORSE RIDING

In Edinburgh itself, Tower Farm Riding Stables, at 85 Liberton Drive by the Braid Hills (tel: 0131-664 3375; www.towerfarm.org), are approved by the Association of British Riding Schools and offer tuition and hacking. A couple of miles beyond the city bypass lessons, hacking and pony trekking are also offered by Edinburgh & Lasswade Riding Centre at Kevock Road, Lasswade (tel: 0131-663 7676; www.lasswadestables.com).

SKATING AND SKIING

Murrayfield Ice Rink (tel: 0131-337 6933; www.murrayfieldicerinkltd.co.uk) is a popular venue for skaters throughout the year, with skate hire available and sessions in the afternoons, evenings and at weekends. Nearby is the Murrayfield Curling Rink, showcasing one of Scotland's national sports (the British Ladies Team, usually all Scots, regularly win medals at the Winter Olympics).

The Snowsports Centre (tel: 0131-445 4433; www.midlothian.gov.uk/info/200281/snowsports_centre; Mon–Fri 9.30am–9pm, Sun 9.30am–

Horseracing at Musselburgh.

7pm) is situated at Hillend on the Biggar Road, half an hour by bus or car from the city centre. Features include Europe's longest artificial slope, sliding in giant tubes, alpine lodge and restaurant, skiing and snowboarding tuition and equipment hire.

SWIMMING POOLS AND SPORTS CENTRES

Edinburgh Leisure (tel: 0131-458 2100; www.edinburghleisure.co.uk) manages the city's numerous sports facilities, of which the following is a selection of some of the best. Note that booking is recommended, particularly in the summer months.

The Royal Commonwealth Pool, at 21 Dalkeith Road (tel: 0131-667 7211) south of the centre, was built for the 1970 Commonwealth Games, and has a gym with weight-training facilities, soft play area and an Olympic-sized pool. The best older (mostly Victorian) swim centres are to be found at Glenogle in Stockbridge (Glenogle Road; tel: 0131-343 6376), Leith (Junction Place; tel: 0131-555 4728), and Portobello (57 The Promenade; tel: 0131-669 6888), which offers authentic Turkish baths.

For tennis and other racket sports, try Craiglockhart Leisure and Tennis Centre (177 Colinton Road; tel: 0131-443 0101), which has 14 indoor and outdoor courts. For football practice and a variety of indoor games, the Jack Kane Sports Centre (208 Niddrie Mains Road; tel: 0131-669 0404) has good facilities. Meadowbank Sports Centre, the sports facility known for hosting the Commonwealth Games twice, is currently closed for a £46 million revamp to be unveiled in 2020.

Spectator Sports

Edinburgh has two Scottish Premier League football clubs, Heart of Midlothian (Hearts; tel: 0333 043 1874; www.heartsfc.co.uk), who have their ground at Tynecastle at the west end of the city, and Hibernian (Hibs; tel: 0131-661 2159; www.hibernianfc.co.uk), playing at Easter Road at the east end. There are matches usually on Saturdays and Wednesdays throughout the season (Aug–May). Rugby internationals are held between January and March at Murrayfield Stadium off Corstorphine Road (Roseburn Street; tel: 0131-346 5000; www.scottishrugby.org), an impressive international arena holding nearly 70,000 people. In the horse racing calendar, around 28 Flat and National Hunt meets are held throughout the year at Musselburgh Racecourse (tel: 0131-665 2859; www.musselburgh-racecourse.co.uk).

FISHING

There are many well-stocked rivers and reservoirs close to the city, and brown trout is found in the Water of Leith (season is from April to September; permit required). Sea angling is possible on the Firth of Forth. Fishing tackle shops, such as Gamefish at 4 Howe Street (www.gamefishltd.co.uk), will advise on regulations, places to fish and techniques, and you can also go to the outdoor activities at www.visitscotland.com.

Themed Holidays

Themed breaks in Edinburgh most often involve exploring art galleries, architecture, or golf courses – but the unusual options below may make you think of extending your stay.

ART

Edinburgh's thriving art scene, associated with home-grown artists such as Henry Raeburn and a plethora of national and private galleries dotted around the city, can be appreciated to an even fuller extent by taking a weekly summer course at the Leith School of Art (25 North Junction Street; tel 0131-554 5671; www.leithschoolofart.co.uk). Enjoy a week of creative inspiration choosing from classes such as figure drawing, still life and printmaking. There are also courses for young artists aged 11–15 years. Throughout the year, weekend workshops are available, too.

COOKERY

If you've missed the workshops at the renowned Edinburgh Food Festival, usually held every year in August, you can now learn, unusually, professional Thai cooking skills at the city's Krua Thai Cookery School (19 Liberton Brae; tel: 0131-664 3036; www.kruathai.co.uk), which offers award-winning courses for professional and amateur chefs in high-quality Thai cuisine, as well as the chance to learn Thai culinary disciplines such as fruit and vegetable carving. Edinburgh School of Food & Wine (The Coach House, Newliston; tel: 0131-333 5001; www.esfw.com) also offers holiday cooking courses, but many are aimed at children needing amusement outside of school.

SPA HOLIDAYS

With the city's selection of fine hotels and long tradition of hospitality, Edinburgh offers an especially good selection of spa breaks. One of the best known is the Balmoral Spa (Balmoral Hotel, 1 Princes Street, which features a pool, sauna, Turkish steam room, gym, and therapies from Indian head massage and full-body massage with hot stones to seaweed body wraps. Spa packages are available. Another superb choice is the One Spa at the Sheraton Hotel (tel: 0131-221 7777; www.onespa.com), which offers an array of relaxation-inducing treatments.

Relaxation guaranteed at the luxurious Balmoral Spa.

Practical Information

GETTING THERE

By Train

Edinburgh Waverley and Edinburgh Haymarket stations service incoming trains. For current fares and timetables, and also for credit-card sales and reservations; tel: 03457-48 49 50; www.nationalrail.co.uk. London North Eastern Railway (www.lner.co.uk) operates hourly services between London Kings Cross and Edinburgh Waverley. The 4 hour 30 minute service is popular, and reservations are recommended. ScotRail also operate a nightly Caledonian Sleeper Service from London, as well as the Spirit of Scotland travel pass, giving unlimited travel on Scotland's rail and ferry networks for 8 or 15 consecutive days; tel: 0344-811 0141; www.scotrail.co.uk.

By Air

Edinburgh International Airport, west of the city on Glasgow Road, is used for regular flights from across the UK and Europe, as well as several transatlantic services. Further flight options are available at Glasgow International and Glasgow Prestwick airports, with good onward public transport connections. Edinburgh Airport Information; tel: 0844-448 8833; www.edinburghairport.com.

By Car

Edinburgh is approached from the south by the A1 coastal road from Berwick-upon-Tweed, the A68 from Jedburgh, and the A7 from Selkirk. There is no motorway route into the southeast of Scotland.

The M6, which travels up the west coast of England, meets with the A74 north of Carlisle, which becomes the M74 and connects with the M8 northeast of Glasgow. Travelling east, the M8 meets with the Edinburgh City bypass, west of Edinburgh. The M8 also connects with the M9 from Stirling at the Newbridge Roundabout, northwest of the city. From the north of Scotland, the M90 now crosses over the Firth of Forth on the Queensferry Crossing, which opened to traffic in 2017, leaving the old road bridge to public transport, cyclists and pedestrians.

By Coach

There are daily and overnight long-distance bus services to St Andrew Square Bus Station from London and elsewhere in the UK. For details, contact National Express (tel: 0871-781 8181; www.nationalexpress.com) or Scottish Citylink (tel: 0871-266 3333; www.citylink.co.uk).

By Sea

Edinburgh's main sea port at Rosyth is now only used for cargo crossings. The nearest sea port for passenger ferries is at Newcastle with sailings to Amsterdam, with DFDS Seaways. Information and bookings, tel: 0871-522 9955; www.dfdsseaways.co.uk.

GETTING AROUND

Public Transport

The main bus company in Edinburgh is Lothian Buses (tel: 0131-555 6363; www.lothianbuses.com), while the First Group (tel: 0345-646 0707; www.firstgroup.com/south-east-and-central-scotland) serves some destinations out of town. You can buy a ticket as you enter the bus (exact change required) or purchase a day ticket, although tickets are not transferable between Lothian and First bus services. Timetables, fares and route information are posted at the main bus stops; night buses operate along all major routes.

Edinburgh's trams (tel: 0131-475 0177; www.edinburghtrams.com), in partnership with Lothian Buses, run for 16 stops between York Place in the New Town and Edinburgh Airport. Tickets must be bought from vending machines at each stop, before you get on the tram.

Going Green

Bicycles are well used across the city, and there are numerous cycle routes. For more information see www.cycle-route.com or www.spokes.org.uk.

Trains

Trains to and from Glasgow take around 50 minutes and run about every 10 minutes between 6am–8pm (and otherwise every 30 minutes), from Haymarket and Waverley stations. National Rail enquiries; tel: 03457-48 49 50; www.nationalrail.co.uk.

Edinburgh Waverley, the city's main railway station.

Driving

Numerous one-way systems and crowded Old Town streets make travelling by car within the city centre a daunting prospect and not recommended for those unfamiliar with Edinburgh. The centre is also quite compact and easily negotiated on foot or by bus and bicycle. That said, a car is very useful for exploring surrounding districts and countryside.

Parking is available all over the city, with major car parks at the top of Leith Street (Omni Centre) and at Holyrood Road. The Waverley Car Park is located at 6 New Street, behind Waverley Station. NCP also operate a car park at Castle Terrace, off Lothian Road. Street parking in the city centre is only permitted within bays marked by white dotted lines, for which you must purchase tickets from metres priced at ten-minute intervals for anything up to 3 hours. There are seven park and ride buses in and around the city, reducing both the cost and the carbon footprint.

Car rental:

Arnold Clark; tel: 0141-237 4374; www.arnoldclarkrental.com

Avis; tel: 0344-544 6059; www.avis.co.uk

Europcar; tel: 0871-384 9900; www.europcar.co.uk

Hertz; tel: 0843-309 3026; www.hertz.co.uk

Taxis

Taxi ranks are located throughout the city centre, notably outside Waverley and Haymarket Stations, the Caledonian Hotel at the West End of Princes Street, and beside the Playhouse Theatre at the top of Leith Walk. Edinburgh's black cabs operate 24 hours. Taxi firms include: Central Taxis, tel: 0131-229 2468; City Cabs, tel: 0131-228 1211; ComCab, tel: 0131-272 8000.

Bicycles

Bikes can be hired from:

Bike Trax 11 Lochrin Place, Tollcross; tel: 0131-228 6633; www.biketrax.co.uk

Cycle Scotland 29 Blackfriars Street; tel: 0131-556 5560; www.cyclescotland.co.uk

Edinburgh Bicycle Co-op 8 Alvanley Terrace, Whitehouse Loan; tel: 0131-331 5010; www.edinburghbicycle.com.

FACTS FOR THE VISITOR

Disabled Travellers

For accessibility information in the city, contact Lothian Centre for Inclusive Living (tel: 0131-475 2350; www.lothiancil.org.uk; Mon–Fri 10am–4pm).

For a largely Georgian/Victorian city, Edinburgh is remarkably well equipped for those with disabilities, and buses and taxis are fitted with ramps for wheelchair users. Many taxis carry a wheelchair symbol. With a few exceptions, most public buildings and hotels have wheelchair facilities, and there are rigid conditions for new building. Private bed and breakfasts vary; contact individual premises. For further advice or support, contact Capability Scotland, tel: 0131-337 9876; www.capability-scotland.org.uk.

Emergencies

Police, ambulance, fire brigade: 999 (for emergencies only).

Police Scotland: 101 (for non-emergencies).

Edinburgh's two major hospitals are the Royal Infirmary of Edinburgh (with Accident & Emergency department), in the Little France suburb (tel: 0131-536 1000) and the Western General Hospital, on Crewe Road South (tel: 0131-537 1000).

Opening Hours

Standard business hours are Mon–Sat 9am–5.30pm, though you will find many premises opening at 10am and/or closing at 6pm, with late shopping (especially in malls) on Thursdays until 8pm. Public holidays are: New Year's Day, 2 January, Good Friday, the first Monday in May, the last Monday in May, the first Monday in August, St Andrew's Day (30 November – or the following Monday, if the 30th falls on a weekend) and 25 and 26 December.

Tourist Information

The Tourist Information Centre is located on top of Waverley Mall at the east end of Princes Street, above Waverley Station. Open June–Aug Mon–Sat 9am–7pm, Sun 10am–7pm (June until 6pm), Sept–May Mon–Sat 9am–5pm, Sun 10am–5pm. Tel: 0131-473 3868; www.visitscotland.com.

Staff can assist with accommodation, bookings and ticket sales, and there is a shop selling souvenirs, maps and guidebooks. A bureau de change and on-line information facility are also located here. There is also a branch of this information desk at Edinburgh Airport (daily 7.30am–7pm).

Scottish Money

The monetary unit is the pound sterling: £1 = 100 pence. Notes issued by the Bank of Scotland, Royal Bank of

National Library of Scotland.

Scotland, and Clydesdale Bank (same value and size, different designs) are standard, while Bank of England notes and coins are also in circulation. Scottish notes are legal currency throughout Britain.

Postal and Internet Services

The main city post office is located in the Waverley Mall, Waverley Bridge (Mon–Sat 9am–5.30pm). Other city-centre post offices are at 40 Frederick Street and 33 Forrest Road (near the University). Internet access hotspots are widely available. For onsite computers and printing services, try Coffee Home Internet Café (28 Crichton Place, Leith Walk; tel: 0131-477 8336; www.coffeehome.co.uk). The National Library on George IV Bridge has free computer access, but you may need to pre-book.

Walking Tours

A plethora of entertaining guided walking tours take place day and night around the Old Town: for evening underground or ghost themed tours, see page 31; literary tours, see page 25; for daytime history tours, contact Mercat (tel: 0131-225 5445; www.mercattours.com), featuring storytelling in atmospheric closes and underground vaults; or the Scottish Storytelling Centre (see page 35). Tourist Tracks tours offer well-informed downloadable city guides for your mobile phone, MP3 player or iPod to guide you on a two-hour audio walk taking in the major sites (www.tourist-tracks.com).

Tipping

Most restaurants do not add a service charge to the bill, and it is usual, but not compulsory, to give a 10–15 percent tip. If a service charge is included, you are not expected to pay extra, unless you wish to reward exceptional service. A tip of at least £1 is appropriate for porters, and it is normal to give taxi drivers 10 percent; however, it is not necessary to tip in self-service establishments or pubs.

Accommodation

As the major UK destination after London, Edinburgh attracts travellers of all descriptions and offers accommodation ranging from cheap to more luxurious hostels, numerous guesthouses and bed and breakfasts, alongside international hotel chains and locally owned boutique properties.

Most visitors will want to stay close to the Old and New Towns, with most upper-end properties located around the Royal Mile or in the Georgian terraces north of Princes Street, and a good number of hostels are also centrally located. More moderate choices are to be found between the West End of Princes Street and Haymarket, and around London Road. Bed and breakfasts are scattered all over the city as well as in Tollcross, Fountainbridge and Marchmont. Staying in Leith is a cheaper option and can be very good value, with excellent restaurants nearby and good bus connections to the centre (10–15 mins). Reasonably priced seasonal accommodation is also available in the halls and self-catering flats of the universities.

Advance booking is essential in the summer months, and particularly during August, when the city is filled to maximum capacity.

The price-codes listed in this section are based on a standard double room for one night in peak season, but outside of the August Festival Season, when prices double or treble. Out-of-season prices can be 50 percent lower. Breakfast is normally included, except in some high-end establishments:

£££ = over £250
££ = £150–250
£ = under £150

Balmoral Hotel interior.

OLD TOWN AND AROUND

Apex Grassmarket Hotel
31–35 Grassmarket; tel: 0131-516 5507; www.apexhotels.co.uk.
In a clear sign of how far the Grassmarket has come, this smart and exclusive property just below the castle is close to the best nightlife and has excellent views, a rooftop restaurant and onsite parking. ££

Inn on the Mile
82 High Street; tel: 0131-556 9940; www.theinnonthemile.co.uk.
Nine lovely boutique bedrooms in a stunning former bank built in 1923 and located near the castle. Breakfast and other meals are taken in the pub on the ground floor. ££

Radisson Collection Royal Mile
1 George IV Bridge; tel: 0131-220 6666; www.radissoncollection.com.
The location couldn't be better for this five-star contemporary hotel. Audaciously designed to the last detail, the hotel oozes glamour, with impressive views of the city and an award-winning Italian restaurant. £££

Ten Hill Place
10 Hill Place; tel: 0131-662 2080; www.tenhillplace.com.
Situated behind the historic Surgeons' Hall, this place has rooms that are spacious, luxurious and well designed with deep colours and wood panelling. ££

NEW TOWN AND AROUND

24 Royal Terrace
24 Royal Terrace; tel: 0131-297 2424; www.24royalterrace.co.uk.

A great place for lovers of contemporary art, with ever-changing pictures adorning the walls of this sumptuous Georgian townhouse in a quiet street near Calton Hill. ££

21212

3 Royal Terrace; tel: 0131-523 1030; www.21212restaurant.co.uk.

Above one of the city's most exclusive (Michelin-starred) restaurants are four of its best rooms. With views up Calton Hill or towards the Water of Leith, each room is furnished with a mix of antique and modern, with subtle lighting and luxurious bathrooms you'll want to spend hours in. £££

Balmoral Hotel

1 Princes Street; tel: 0131-556 2414; www.roccofortehotels.com.

Edinburgh's classic, big five-star hotel sits imposingly at the eastern end of Princes Street. Expect excellent service, an award-winning spa, sublime restaurants and a luxurious atmosphere. £££

The Edinburgh Lodge

6 Hampton Terrace, West Coates; tel: 0131-337 3682; www.edinburgh lodge.co.uk.

Small, elegant and family-run establishment close to Haymarket Station. Reliably offering good service and local advice. Traditionally furnishings, plus a small garden. ££

The Edinburgh Residence

7 Rothesay Terrace; tel: 0131-226 3380; www.theedinburghresidence.com.

Enjoy luxury with a difference comprising 29 suites in a townhouse in the West End. Dine in the privacy of your own suite, take drinks in the elegant drawing room or self-cater with your room's microwave and minibar. ££

Elder York Guesthouse

38 Elder Street; tel: 0131-556 1926; www.elderyork.co.uk.

Lovely family-run guesthouse in a central location offering a superb full Scottish breakfast, and great value. Be aware that there are a lot of stairs and no lift. £

The Principal Charlotte Square

38 Charlotte Square; tel: 0131-341 5136; www.phcompany.com/princi pal/edinburgh-charlotte-square.

On Edinburgh's grandest square, this smart hotel is housed in seven interconnecting Georgian townhouses. Breakfast is taken in the stunning inner courtyard. £££

OUTSIDE OF THE CITY CENTRE AND SUBURBS

A-Haven Townhouse

180 Ferry Road; tel: 0131-554 6559; www.a-haven.co.uk.

Good breakfasts, a hotel bar, garden and assorted household oddments make this 14-room place ia quirky option. Near the Botanic Garden. £

Malmaison Edinburgh

1 Tower Place, Leith; tel: 0131-285 1478; www.malmaison.com.

A superb renovation of Leith's former Seamen's Mission building featuring Art Deco styling, four-poster beds and a brasserie with views over the port. ££

Prestonfield House Hotel

Priestfield Road; tel: 0131-225 7800; www.prestonfield.com.

Old-world charm in a 17th-century mansion just 10 minutes from the city centre. The location combined with a fine-dining restaurant and lavish decor, makes this a real treat. £££

The Thistle House

1 Kilmaurs Terrace; tel: 0131-667 2002; www.thethistlehouse.co.uk.

Good B&B serving a fine breakfast, with attentive service. Most accommodation is en suite. ££

Thrums Hotel

14–15 Minto Street; tel: 0131-667 5545; www.thrumshotel.com.

This great-value guesthouse a mile from the city centre maintains some period furnishings to match the Georgian architecture. Rooms are minimal but comfortable, and there's a private garden and parking. £